Taking a Serious God Seriously

D1714615

James Perry

Taking a Serious God Seriously

Library of Congress Control Number: 2011939845

ISBN 9780983244158

DEDICATION

Prior to my meeting a very special person who would become my wife (Peggy Ann Fry), there were three other women who made a lasting impression upon me.

Two of the people mentioned in this Dedication (my Mother and Grandmother) will not be privy to it, inasmuch as they died a few years ago. However, they made a lasting impression and were a firm influence upon me. I would be remiss if I failed to remember and honor them.

The first was my Mother, Barbara S. Perry, who became a widow in 1941 and the sole caregiver for her three children. Out of this necessity, she found employment in a Bank. I never recall any complaint from her in this regard. My Mother was able to see me graduate from College and Seminary, as well as to visit in two of the Churches where I was privileged to be the Pastor. It was obvious that she was proud of her youngest child's achievements.

The second woman who was willing to help care for my brother, my sister and me, her Mother (our Grandmother), Isabella MacLean Smith, moved in with us. She had come to this country from Scotland in the early 1900s where she had a strict religious background and was frequent in her quoting Scripture to us, along with pithy and pointed statements intended to guide us on a right path. The impression and influence she had upon me has served me well over the years. I remember her comment made often to me as I was headed out of the home – "Remember, thou God seest me!" Regrettably, she died in 1948.

The third woman who has been special in my life is my favorite sister – Ruth P. Kuttruf. Ruth has always been close to me both as a sister and friend. She is a very special person who has endured and overcome much in her life. She did not let that deter her from being stalwart in doing the best she could whenever she could. Ruth has always been an encouragement to me.

A passage of God's Word under the paragraph title: The Woman Who Fears the Lord - Proverbs 31:27-28 - has application in this Dedication that honors three women: "She looks well to the ways of her household and does not eat the bread of idleness. Her children rise up and call her blessed…" I praise God for my Mother, Grandmother and Sister who selflessly made a difference in my life.

Foreword

There should be a determined purpose to make certain that God is pleased with all of our thoughts and deeds, as well as in the manner by which we acknowledge Him always and in all things. This is how the behavior must be for the one who is Taking A Serious God Seriously. Also, this is doubtlessly the reason why Jesus taught His followers about the necessity for a behavior that will maximize one's fullest realization of being In Christ and His being in us.

In John 15:1-14, Jesus teaches: "...Abide in me, and I in you. As the branch cannot bear fruit by itself, unless it abides in the vine, neither can you, unless you abide in me. I am the vine; you are the branches. Whoever abides in me and I in him, he it is that bears much fruit, for apart from me you can do nothing..." Jesus goes on to amplify this walk and relationship when He states: "If you abide in me, and my words abide in you, ask whatever you wish, and it will be done for you. By this my Father is glorified, that you bear much fruit and so prove to be my disciples." He also indicates a complete and mutual reality in Vs. 11, "These things I have spoken to you, that my joy may be in you, and that your joy may be full."

This is that which occurs for everyone who will purpose to be Taking A Serious God Seriously. I trust that the following pages will assist each of you as you seek an ever-closer walk and fellowship with your God and Savior.

Table of Contents

Introduction

No one knows or is able to predict when the Bridegroom will appear and walk in the midst of His bride – The Church. For the one Taking A Serious God Seriously, there will be the expectation and preparation for his soon appearing. When one believes the Holy Scriptures, there are certain truths that are clear: (1) Jesus Christ is coming again; (b) He's coming on a day and at an hour that no one knows or is able to predict; (c) when He returns, there will be an assessment of His Church similar to Revelation 2 and 3; (d) it will be a time of both surprise and disappointment; (e) for those surprised, it will mean reward – for those disappointed, it will mean banishment from His Kingdom.

The basis by which there will be both surprise and disappointment is stated in Matthew 7:21-23, "Not everyone who says to me, 'Lord, Lord,' will enter the kingdom of heaven, but the one who does the will of my Father who is in heaven. On that day many will say to me, 'Lord, Lord, did we not prophesy in your name, and cast out demons in your name, and do many mighty works in your name?' And then will I declare to them, I never knew you; depart from me, you workers of lawlessness." A second passage is Matthew 25:31-46, "...When the Son of Man comes in his glory, and all the angels with him, then he will sit on his glorious throne. Before him will be gathered all the nations, and he will separate people one from another as a shepherd separates the sheep from the goats...Then the King will say to those on his right, 'Come, you who are blessed by my Father, inherit the kingdom prepared for you from the foundation of the world... Then he will say to those on his left, 'Depart from me, you cursed, into the eternal fire prepared for the devil and his angels...And these will go away into eternal punishment, but the righteous into eternal life." A third passage is II Thessalonians 2:7-12, "For the mystery of lawlessness is already at work. Only he who now restrains it will do so until he is out of the way. And then the lawless one will be revealed, whom the Lord Jesus will kill with the breath of his mouth and bring to nothing by the appearance of his coming. The coming of the lawless one is by the activity of Satan with all power and false signs and wonders, and with all wicked deception for those who are perishing, because they refused to love the truth and so be saved. Therefore God sends them a strong delusion, so that they may believe what is false, 12 in order that all may be condemned who did not believe the truth but had pleasure in unrighteousness."

The Holy Scriptures are clear that drastic and catastrophic times are on the horizon. It is a time that should stimulate and provoke thorough and serious self-examination. It is a time to ascertain whether or not you will be numbered with the sheep or goats. The people in Noah's day discovered that once the rain started to fall and they rushed to gain entrance into the Ark of Refuge – they had waited too long and missed their opportunity for safety and deliverance.

You have this moment! This is your day! The opportunity to get into a right and meaningful relationship with The Good Shepherd may not pass your way again. Whatever you do, make some time and space where you can purpose that you will begin Taking A Serious God Seriously. It will be the decisive time when you will either be numbered with the sheep or numbered with the goats. Your soul and eternity are at a threshold decision point. Take that step of faith now!

Rumbling and Crumbling

The approach to the Twenty-First Century came with many concerns – would the computerized power grids adjust and reprogram themselves at Midnight on December 31, 1999 and smoothly transition and begin the January 01, 2000 free of any glitch or malfunction; would the financial structures adjust and adapt to a new century; etc. Someone developed a list of the 10 major global concerns of the 21st Century. Among them were: (a) Individual Abuse Among Human Beings – Abuse and Bullying are occurring with regularity throughout the world; (b) Economic Manipulation and False Shortages – It would entail manipulating markets and commodities in such a way as to create shortages that drive prices higher certainly increase sales and profits, but also lead to deaths of innocent people; (c) Unjust Wars – the increase of unrest among populations with a heart cry to be free (without a clear understanding of what true freedom really is; (d) Oil – the dependency upon and increasing consumption of oil; (e) Terrorism – The constancy of threats and the activity using Bombs to make a statement and to strike fear into the hearts of the citizens of the world; etc.

As this Century closed its first decade, there was also the phenomena of upheavals in the culture and nature. The nation was shocked, mesmerized and grieved by terrorists commandeering airliners on 09-11-2001 and crashing two into the World Trade Center in New York City; one into the Pentagon in Washington, D. C.; and a fourth plane that was headed toward The Capital or The White House except for the brave and sacrificial acts of those on that flight who took control of the aircraft but with the result that it was crashed in Shanksville, PA. On the other hand, there was the increased severity and activity In nature - typhoons, tsunamis, tornadoes, earthquakes in unusual places (5.8 magnitude that impacted from Virginia up to and into Canada), hurricanes with considerable damage due to high winds and flooding, etc.

To say that we are living in astonishing times is an understatement. Events are moving at such a rapid pace making it impossible for one to pause for a breath of air before another major event occurs. People do not know how to explain their feelings or what is happening around them. They are like a boat that has lost its mooring and is just drifting with the tide, waves and winds. The Foundations of the World, Church and Individual Lives are Rumbling, Crumbling and Tumbling. Where will it all end? What is the Hope and Expectation for the future? Is there a prophetic and spiritual approach and interpretation for these times in which we live? Can the activity within nature be predicted or is it something that 'just happens' in the grand theme of life?

An illustration and instance of this occurred on Friday, March 11, 2011 – just another day of normal activity in Japan – until the earth started to move strangely beneath one's feet; walls started to vibrate; buildings began to shake; items on store shelves began to be shaken off their display – and the reality of a 9.0 earthquake started. The earthquake was so powerful that it moved Honshu 2.4 meters (7.9 feet) East and shifted the Earth on its axis by almost 10 cm (3.9 inches). The World Bank, on March 21st, estimated damage between $122 Billion and $235 Billion. Compounding matters even further, the Earthquake was followed by a Tsunami Wave that at points reached a height of 33 feet. What was not shaken apart and destroyed was caught up in the Tsunami and swept away. Close to 18,000 people were unaccounted for and rescue operations seem to leave little hope that survivors will be found. The Tsunami had an additional impact on four Nuclear Power Plants where power needed for cooling was unavailable and radiation leakage had begun. People were urged to relocate between twenty and fifty miles away from the radiation leaks. A normal day became a day of loss, desperation, death, and uncertainty.

Also, on April 27th, 2011 a tornado swept through several areas and leaving areas in Tuscaloosa, AL completely in ruins. The news reports recorded: "An extremely large and violent tornado outbreak, the largest tornado outbreak ever recorded, and popularly known as the 2011 Super Outbreak, occurred from April 25 to 28, 2011. The outbreak affected the Southern, Midwestern, and Northeastern United States, leaving catastrophic destruction in its wake – especially across the State of Alabama. It produced destructive tornadoes in Alabama, Arkansas, Georgia, Mississippi, North Carolina, South Carolina, Tennessee, Virginia - and affected several other areas throughout the Southern and Eastern United States. At least 336 tornadoes were confirmed as of August 4, 2011 by the National Weather Service in 21 states from Texas to New York and even isolated tornadoes in Canada. Widespread and destructive tornadoes occurred on each day of the outbreak, with April 27, 2011 being among the most prolific and destructive tornado days in United States history. Four of the tornadoes were destructive enough to be rated EF5 on the Enhanced Fujita Scale, which is the highest ranking possible; typically these tornadoes are only recorded about once each year or less. In total, an estimated 346 people were killed as a result of the outbreak..."

As the world's horizon becomes cluttered with earthquakes, floods, tornadoes, revolution in Middle Eastern countries, economic peril, escalating prices and many things that are both unpredictable and yet unknown, what should one do to plan for such phenomena? . The Headlines from April 17th, 2011 give a frightening report regarding 267 Tornadoes reported and 241 touching down in the span of three days. The report from Yahoo News summarizes: "From Thursday, April 14, 2011 to Saturday, April, 16, 2011, devastating tornadoes rampaged across communities of the southern United States. Cities and towns from Oklahoma to North Carolina were assaulted by the deadly twisters. The tornado outbreak led to a total of 267 tornado reports in 15 states over the three-day period. This will likely rank this tornado outbreak among the largest in history. Tragically, the death toll has risen to 45 people so far with dozens of others injured." Then the unexpected happened across several Southern States when a powerful Tornado swept across and wreaked havoc in its path. Alabama was hard hit and hundreds of people are recorded as dead. The count keeps increasing as some of the missing are found. Many people's homes were completely destroyed. Businesses were shattered and became little more than debris. Some of them were uninsured and the losses are immeasurable.

It appears that the intensity of Earthquakes, Volcanoes, Tornadoes and Hurricanes has increased, and Tsunami Waves are becoming more of a reality throughout the world. How should these unfolding events be understood? What accounts for such dramatic changes and swift destruction? Some raise the question: "Is God angry and sending His judgment upon those who have ignored Him for so long? Is God trying to get the attention of people around the World? Is this a dramatic and powerful warning from God to get people to return to Him and to seek Him?

Some seize the moment to claim it is due to Global Warming, whereas others embrace in their belief system that it is all part of the Doomsday Prophecies articulated in the Holy Scriptures. Many immediately go to the words of Jesus in Matthew 24:6-8, "...you will hear of wars and rumors of wars. See that you are not alarmed, for this must take place, but the end is not yet. For nation will rise against nation, and kingdom against kingdom, and there will be famines and earthquakes in various places. All these are but the beginning of the birth pains..." The news about natural disasters - earthquakes and Tsunamis in Japan, and the political events rapidly unfolding in the Middle East and North Africa – cause one to wonder about the bigger picture – the eternal plan of The Almighty God and His reaction and response to man's disregard of Him and His Creation.

Then - on the night of May 1st, 2011 news alerts were given to the media that the President of the United States had an important announcement regarding national security to make to the nation and the world at 10:30 PM. The usual delays ensued and it was almost Midnight before the President addressed the nation. By the time he got to the cameras and microphones, the news speculators had come to the conclusion that the announcement would inform all that Osama bin Laden had been killed by a United States Special Forces Unit in Pakistan. There was a mixture of glee and gloating because the acclaimed architect of September 11th, 2001 had been flushed out, offered the opportunity to surrender, refused and was killed in the firefight that followed. The President's brief address included that "justice has been done." However – is this a time for glee and gloating – or – for sober reflection in terms of who or what we are and/or have become? For many, this was the occasion to celebrate. For others, they were in the midst of their own tragedy following the horrific Tornado that ripped across the South and wreaked major loss in the State of Alabama.

Osama bin Laden has symbolized the age of terrorism in which the world finds itself. This symbol has occupied the attention of three American administrations – Presidents William J. Clinton; George W. Bush and Barack H. Obama. The comments of the former Presidents is telling. President Clinton, who was in office for the first World Trade Center bombing in 1993, issued a written statement: "I congratulate the President, the National Security team and the members of our armed forces on bringing Osama bin Laden to justice after more than a decade of murderous al-Qaida attacks..." Former President George W. Bush, whose entire presidency was defined by the September 11th attacks, said in a statement that President Obama called him to inform him of the news of bin Laden's death. Bush called the operation a "momentous achievement that marks a victory for America, for people who seek peace around the world, and for all those who lost loved ones on September 11, 2001: I congratulated him and the men and women of our military and intelligence communities who devoted their lives to this mission. They have our everlasting gratitude...The fight against terror goes on, but tonight America has sent an unmistakable message: No matter how long it takes, justice will be done."

What should one's perspective be in these rapidly changing times and amidst these stupendous events in both the creation as a whole and nations in particular? In Amos 3:3-11, The Lord speaks and asks some rhetorical questions – and the prophet records these words: "Do two walk together, unless they have agreed to meet? Does a lion roar in the forest, when he has no prey? Does a young lion cry out from his den, if he has taken nothing? Does a bird fall in a snare on the earth, when there is no trap for it?...Is a trumpet blown in a city, and the people are not afraid? Does disaster come to a city, unless the Lord has done it? For the Lord God does nothing without revealing his secret to his servants the prophets. The lion has roared; who will not fear? The Lord God has spoken; who can but prophesy? Proclaim to the strongholds in Ashdod and to the strongholds in the land of Egypt, and say, Assemble yourselves on the mountains of Samaria, and see the great tumults within her, and the oppressed in her midst. They do not know how to do right, declares the Lord, those who store up violence and robbery in their strongholds. Therefore thus says the Lord God: An adversary shall surround the land and bring down your defenses from you, and your strongholds shall be plundered." In the midst of this prophecy are these words: "Does disaster come to a city, unless the Lord has done it?"

Does God respond with cataclysmic events in the world and upheavals among the peoples of the earth? There are some Biblical events that can give one some helpful guidance. The first is in Chapters 6 through 9 of Genesis. This is the account of Noah and the events leading up to the flood. The crux of the matter is in Genesis 6:5-9, "The Lord saw how great man's wickedness on the earth had become, and that every inclination of the thoughts of his heart was only evil all the time. The Lord was grieved that he had made man on the earth, and his heart was filled with pain. So the Lord said, I will wipe mankind, whom I have created, from the face of the earth--men and animals, and creatures that move along the ground, and birds of the air -- for I am grieved that I have made them. But Noah found favor in the eyes of the Lord. This is the account of Noah. Noah was a righteous man, blameless among the people of his time, and he walked with God." Capture the sense of how God felt when He looked upon His creation and saw how mankind was rejecting Him and His desires for them. The Scripture states: "...His heart was filled with pain...I am grieved that I have made them..." How great was that "pain" and how severe was that "grief"? Is there any human way that one can measure it and/or comprehend it? Can one allow the measurement of that pain and grief with the experience of an individual passing through times of difficulty or sorrow? If so, that would be a very low threshold of and for the pain God is indicating and knowing!

In Genesis 18:20-33, there's a scene where God is speaking of His concern because of the sinful behavior of people in the cities of Sodom and Gomorrah. Abraham's interest is due to the fact that his nephew, Lot, resides there with his family. Abraham intercedes on the basis of possible righteous people living in those cities. God, in effect, states: If you can find any righteous there, other than Lot, I will not rain judgment upon those places. Abraham is convinced after much prayer that God's plan for judgment is just. In Genesis 19:13-17, Angels are sent to Lot to inform of his need to gather all who are related to him and flee from those cities. The Word of the Lord is clear: "The outcry to the Lord against its people is so great that he has sent us to destroy it. So Lot went out and spoke to his sons-in-law, who were pledged to marry his daughters. He said, Hurry and get out of this place, because the Lord is about to destroy the city! But his sons-in-law thought he was joking. With the coming of dawn, the angels urged Lot, saying, Hurry! Take your wife and your two daughters who are here, or you will be swept away when the city is punished. When he hesitated, the men grasped his hand and the hands of his wife and of his two daughters and led them safely out of the city, for the Lord was merciful to them. As soon as they had brought them out, one of them said, Flee for your lives! Don't look back, and don't stop anywhere in the plain! Flee to the mountains or you will be swept away!"

A statement appears in Genesis 19 that is so typical of those who hear the Gospel and the message of deliverance in Christ, namely, "But his sons-in-law thought he was joking." This is sadly and too often the response of some who are urged to "Flee from the wrath to come!" – they think it is more a joke than a reality. Their epitaph could well be: "But they thought the messenger was joking." What did God do with Sodom and Gomorrah? Was it all a joke? Genesis 19:24-25 declares it was no joking matter: "Then the Lord rained down burning sulfur on Sodom and Gomorrah - from the Lord out of the heavens. Thus he overthrew those cities and the entire plain, including all those living in the cities - and also the vegetation in the land." The reality is always – God says what He means and means what He says!

One other illustration from among many is found in Numbers 16:23-33 where a penalty will be imposed upon Korah and all of his family and possessions because of their sin and rebellion. The text states: "Then the Lord said to Moses, Say to the assembly, Move away from the tents of Korah, Dathan and Abiram. Moses got up and went to Dathan and Abiram, and the elders of Israel followed him. He warned the assembly, Move back from the tents of these wicked men! Do not touch anything belonging to them, or you will be swept away because of all their sins. So they moved away from the tents of Korah, Dathan and Abiram. Dathan and Abiram had come out and were standing with their wives, children and little ones at the entrances to their tents. Then Moses said, This is how you will know that the Lord has sent me to do all these things and that it was not my idea: If these men die a natural death and experience only what usually happens to men, then the Lord has not sent me. But if the Lord brings about something totally new, and the earth opens its mouth and swallows them, with everything that belongs to them, and they go down alive into the grave, then you will know that these men have treated the Lord with contempt. As soon as he finished saying all this, the ground under them split apart and the earth opened its mouth and swallowed them, with their households and all Korah's men and all their possessions. They went down alive into the grave, with everything they owned; the earth closed over them, and they perished and were gone from the community."

Some actions by the Lord are difficult for people to understand and accept. They eagerly argue that God is a God of Love and Mercy and would never punish people harshly. They question whether or not the servant of the Lord has a clue when they represent the coming judgment of God for sinful behavior and rebellion. This comes from an ignorance about (a) God's Holiness, (b) God's standard of righteousness, and (c) God's Law. Moses states a personal word about the impending judgment when he states: "Moses said, This is how you will know that the Lord has sent me to do all these things and that it was not my idea..." He wants the people to focus upon God. He wants them to understand that God will always accomplish all of His Holy Will. God will never wink at sin and rebellion – nor should we. God will never tolerate the wickedness and evil acts of people – nor should we! God will never deal matter-of-factly with sin at any time – nor should we!

Are the world events merely a hiccup or a shrug in a given moment of time? Have we become totally impervious (incapable of being influenced, persuaded, or affected) to the ways and thoughts of God? Are we at all concerned with God's ways and thoughts? Are we so foolish to believe that man can function with impunity (exemption from punishment...immunity from detrimental effects) and without consequence for his deeds and actions? What if all these current events are a prelude of II Peter 3:10-12, "But the day of the Lord will come like a thief, and then the heavens will pass away with a roar, and the heavenly bodies will be burned up and dissolved, and the earth and the works that are done on it will be exposed. Since all these things are thus to be dissolved, what sort of people ought you to be in lives of holiness and godliness, waiting for and hastening the coming of the day of God, because of which the heavens will be set on fire and dissolved, and the heavenly bodies will melt as they burn!"

It would be desirable to have the sense of David when he wrote in Psalm 77:15-20, "You with your arm redeemed your people, the children of Jacob and Joseph. When the waters saw you, O God...they were afraid; indeed, the deep trembled. The clouds poured out water; the skies gave forth thunder; your arrows flashed on every side. The crash of your thunder was in the whirlwind; your lightning lighted up the world; the earth trembled and shook. Your way was through the sea, your path through the great waters; yet your footprints were unseen. You led your people like a flock by the hand of Moses and Aaron." Sadly, in every generation, there are those whose ears do not hear the roaring and thundering of God; their eyes are blinded to the flashing lightning; and the footprints of the Lord are conveniently unnoticed and unseen. How great is this tragedy for those who choose to ignore the Living God!

Noah quickly learned the purpose and reality of God. He faithfully preached righteousness and the need to flee from the wrath to come – but – he was ridiculed and ignored. However, he tirelessly carried out the task God had given him to do. At God's appointed time, all of what had been declared became the reality and people suddenly knew the ways and thoughts of God. For those inside the ark – it meant refuge, salvation, deliverance. For those outside the ark – it meant the wrath of God, judgment, death. The same truth applied in the situation with Abraham, Lot and the people who resided in Sodom and Gomorrah – God was serious about His message and intent. Time had been given for repentance and change – but it was ignored and rejected. This is the same truth experienced by Korah, Dathan and Abiram – the instant and convincing reality that God will judge both harshly and finality all those who sin and rebel against Him.

The world today has been given the opportunity to flee from wrath to come. The Word of the Lord is clear to all people in all generations. The Lord spoke and we find His Words in II Chronicles 7:13-14, "When I shut up the heavens so that there is no rain, or command locusts to devour the land or send a plague among my people, if my people, who are called by my name, will humble themselves and pray and seek my face and turn from their wicked ways, then will I hear from heaven and will forgive their sin and will heal their land." Again, in Isaiah 55:6-9, "Seek the Lord while he may be found; call on him while he is near. Let the wicked forsake his way and the evil man his thoughts. Let him turn to the Lord, and he will have mercy on him, and to our God, for he will freely (abundantly) pardon. For my thoughts are not your thoughts, neither are your ways my ways, declares the Lord. As the heavens are higher than the earth, so are my ways higher than your ways and my thoughts than your thoughts." The Lord can and will be found by you if you seek for Him with all your heart and soul. He is serious about His plan and His desire for people to repent and turn to Him? Are you/we as serious about spiritual matters as is God? Have you sought Him and called out to Him to forgive your sin? Have you turned from your wicked ways and committed yourself to walk in His ways for your life? Are you eager to know His thoughts and His will for you now and always? Heed the words of the Hymn written by John M. Wigner in 1871 - - -

Come to the Savior now, He gently calleth thee;
In true repentance bow, Before Him bend the knee;
He waiteth to bestow Salvation, peace, and love,
True joy on earth below, A home in Heav'n above.

Come to the Savior now, Ye who have wandered far;
Renew your solemn vow, For His by right you are;
Come, like poor wand'ring sheep Returning to His fold;
His arm will safely keep, His love will ne'er grow cold.

Come to the Savior, all, Whate'er your burdens be;
Hear now His loving call, "Cast all your care on Me."
Come, and for ev'ry grief In Jesus you will find
A sure and safe relief, A loving Friend and kind.

Amen!

This is serious and vital. Come to the Savior NOW is a serious invitation! Finding Him as a Loving Friend and Kind NOW is a serious result! How serious are you with this area of your life with the Lord?

QUESTIONS FOR THOUGHT AND APPLICATION

1. As you consider the world today, do you think it is evolving or eroding? Why?

2. In order for one to Take A Serious God Seriously, what is a Biblical rational for doing so? Is there a standard and purpose given by God in terms of one's relationship to Him?

Consider: Exodus 20:1-9 (NKJV) - - -
And God spoke all these words, saying: I am the Lord your God, who brought you out of the land of Egypt, out of the house of bondage. You shall have no other gods before Me. You shall not make for yourself a carved image, or any likeness of anything that is in heaven above, or that is in the earth beneath, or that is in the water under the earth; you shall not bow down to them nor serve them. For I, the Lord your God, am a jealous God, visiting the iniquity of the fathers on the children to the third and fourth generations of those who hate Me, but showing mercy to thousands, to those who love Me and keep My commandments. You shall not take the name of the Lord your God in vain, for the Lord will not hold him guiltless who takes His name in vain. Remember the Sabbath day, to keep it holy. Six days you shall labor and do all your work, 10 but the seventh day is the Sabbath of the Lord your God. In it you shall do no work...

(a) What does God mean by: "no other gods before Me"?

(b) What are some of the temporal things that can be construed to be "graven images"?

(c) In what ways can one "bow down to" and or serve a temporal god/gods?

(d) How do you understand the word "jealous" when God states that He is "a jealous God"?

(e) What are some of the ways one can take the name of the Lord in vain?

(f) What are some common ways a "professing Christian" takes the name of the Lord in vain?

(g) When one prays "in Jesus' name", what exactly does that state and mean?

(h) Have you ever asked God for comfort and/or peace, and then fretted and worried about the very thing you prayed about and asked for "in Jesus' name"?

3. When it comes to worship of God, have you ever been in attendance or witnessed a "worship service" that was more secular than spiritual?

4. Is the format and structure of a worship service significant as one comes to Take A Serious God Seriously? Why?

5. In John 4:21-24, what was Jesus stating and implying in terms of Worship?

6. What has Jesus stated is the only acceptable approach for true worship?

7. Are the words of Jesus descriptive of your approach and experience in Worship? Why? Why not?

The law of the Lord is perfect, converting the soul;
The testimony of the Lord is sure, making wise the simple;
The statutes of the Lord are right, rejoicing the heart;
The commandment of the Lord is pure, enlightening the eyes...
                                              Psalm 19:7-8 (NKJV)

Societal Irrelevance

When one encounters the unexpected, the unplanned for, the unwanted – what should one do? Where should one turn? When things are so desperate, where can one find help and relief? When the storms of life are so horrendous and in the matter of moments everything is gone, where can one go to find comfort, encouragement, resources, assistance in the immediate and for the longer term? Who will understand? Who will reach out with compassion and genuine care? Is there someone – anyone – somewhere – anywhere – who can and will weep with me while I am weeping?

When Tornadoes and Hurricanes ravage areas, cities, countries – one of the immediate needs for many people is for some drinkable water. Food, shelter, clothing are also vital when the storms have taken away one's human resources – the possessions and provisions that have been accumulated. It is similar to suddenly become naked and the inability to do anything to alleviate that desperate situation and need. Whoever reaches out becomes an immediate friend for one in need. In terms of the need for water, few have had that unbearable experience or need.

An article published by Life Action Ministries – Revival Magazine – contained a reference to this real life experience in the life of a missionary family. The Magazine article is: "Thirsty For Jesus?" One of the great champions for Revival was Dr. Stephen Olford. In a conference, Heart-Cry For Revival held in 1998, Dr. Olford related an incident from his years as a teenager being reared in Central Africa where his parents were missionaries. He recounts: "...my father was making contact with a new tribe. There was no road, not even a trail. On and on our family went, with only a few native people accompanying us. What we didn't realize was that we were moving away from any river. When we ran out of water, my father asked our African guides to find and bring us some. One day went by. A second day went by. On the third day under the blistering sun, we began to really suffer. I'll never forget it. I was a teenager. My tongue was clinging to my jaws. Saliva had gone. My eyes were blistering from the heat. My brother John was delirious. We were thirsty! With the possibility of death staring us in the face, my father drew our family together. Under that absolutely cloudless sky, with the heat and bright sun beating down on us, he said, Let us all kneel. As best I can remember, my father just raised his hand to heaven and said: Father in heaven, in the name of the Lord Jesus Christ, I bow before you. You sent us to this place. I thank You for the translation of Scriptures and the building of churches. If it's the hour of our ultimate sacrifice, we're ready. But, Lord, You're sovereign; You're mighty. You're the God of the impossible. Lord, I cry to You, I plead with You— Lord, send us rain!"

All would readily affirm that this was a desperate moment in the lives of those endeavoring to do pioneer work for the Lord in Africa. Will the Lord forsake His own in the hour and time of need? How relevant is this God Who we profess to love and serve? Was God serious when He issued His promises to His people? Were we serious when we professed faith in Him and committed our lives to Him? Are His promises dependable or are they merely nice sounding clichés? Is there significant meaning to the words that Paul wrote Timothy – II Timothy 2:11-13 – "The saying is trustworthy, for: If we have died with him, we will also live with him; if we endure, we will also reign with him; if we deny him, he also will deny us; if we are faith-less, he remains faithful--for he cannot deny himself." The key phrase is: "He remains faithful – for He cannot deny Himself." In The Message paraphrase – II Timothy 2:11-15 - "This is a sure thing: If we die with him, we'll live with him; If we stick it out with him, we'll rule with him; If we turn our backs on him, he'll turn his back on us; If we give up on him, he does not give up - for there's no way he can be false to himself. Repeat these basic essentials over and over to God's people. Warn them before God against pious nitpicking, which chips away at the faith. It just wears everyone out. Concentrate on doing your best for God..." Is this the God who is your Savior? Is this the confidence you have and practice – God is faithful and will never fail to accomplish His good will for His own!

What happened to the Olford family in Central Africa on that momentous day when they had run out of water and were thirsty for just a drop that would satisfy? Will God answer the prayer of desperate people in their desperate situation? Dr. Olford went on to say: "As God is my witness, in a matter of moments, the clouds began to gather. The sun was shielded, and suddenly there was lightning and a roar of thunder, and a deluge came down. We put out everything we possessed—our canvas, our tub, our wash basin—everything, and we drank, and we drank, and we drank, and we drank. Why? We were thirsty." Dr. Olford went on to make this vital application based upon John 7:37-38, "Are you thirsty like that for Jesus? Jesus said, "If anyone thirsts, let him come to Me and drink. He who believes in Me, as the Scripture has said, Out of his heart shall flow rivers of living water."

In the human dilemma, usually the first responders are The Red Cross and The Salvation Army. While they can assist, their resources are limited by the donations they receive. This factor limits the amount of the help they can offer. In the case of the Tuscaloosa Alabama Tornado on April 27th, 2011, The Salvation Army local building and office was hit by the Storm and is itself devastated and needing to be rebuilt. However, to their credit, they were able to function with several Mobile Units that served the needs of many. State Government can offer some assistance, but it is also limited to emergency funds that are available at the time of a major calamity and emergency, as well as to the scope in terms of an area that has been suddenly impacted. FEMA (Federal Emergency Management Agency) can offer some financial relief but it is limited to the enormity of the area of need as well as to the resources that are available. It seems as though in the time of greatest need one is further frustrated by the limited assistance available and the time delays before any help or relief is offered and given.

Some Churches responded very well with their mobilization of work crews and basic supplies for those most greatly impacted by the Tornado's devastation. Some opened up their facilities to provide shelter for those whose homes are just another pile of rubble. While a large percentage of "Christian" people tend toward generosity, the response is somewhat limited by the economics of a given day, as well as by the debt levels being serviced by both the "Church" in terms of mortgages and the individual in terms of personal debt management (usually caused by over-extension of credit card debt). How much can a "Church" or an individual do to help alleviate both the physical and spiritual needs of those who have been impacted so greatly?

There is a scene recorded in the Gospels about Jesus and His disciples on a boat when a storm (a sudden squall) broke out. It is recorded in Mark 4:35-41; Luke 8:22-25 and Matthew 8:18-27. The interesting Biblical text account is – Mark 4:35-41 – inasmuch as Mark includes one detail that Matthew and Luke omit. Mark records: "That day when evening came, he said to his disciples, Let us go over to the other side. Leaving the crowd behind, they took him along, just as he was, in the boat. There were also other boats with him. A furious squall came up, and the waves broke over the boat, so that it was nearly swamped. Jesus was in the stern, sleeping on a cushion. The disciples woke him and said to him, Teacher, don't you care if we drown? He got up, rebuked the wind and said to the waves, Quiet! Be still! Then the wind died down and it was completely calm. He said to his disciples, Why are you so afraid? Do you still have no faith? They were terrified and asked each other, Who is this? Even the wind and the waves obey him!" The detail that Mark includes is in Verse 35 – "There were also other boats with him." We can characterize these other little boats as people who are caught in the storms of life.

We need to note the concern and action of the disciples. Some of these men spent most of their lives on boats as fishermen and they knew the potential of the storm and sudden squall – they knew that this was a serious matter and their lives depended on what they did. In part, they did the right thing – they came to Jesus and asked Him for some help. It may have been that they wanted Him to man an oar or help to bail water from the vessel – but at least – they came to Jesus. We can only sense that their voices must have quivered because of their excitement and fear of imminent death. They may even have wondered whether or not Jesus was relevant for their need and in the on-going situation! Does Jesus care about us – about me? They come to Jesus – "Jesus was in the stern, sleeping on a cushion. The disciples woke him and said to him, Teacher, don't you care if we drown?" This is a serious and very desperate moment for these men – "Don't You care if we drown (or perish)?" Was Jesus serious about all of what He had taught them about putting all their faith and confidence in Him?

The question is, for whom were the disciples concerned – who is included in the "we" when they spoke of drowning? Was it just those on the boat with Jesus, or did it include the other little boats that were tossing about in the troubled sea? Did they know who was in "the other little boats"? Were they true believers, or seekers, or just the curious? Had the disciples cared? Does Jesus care about the occupants of the "other little boats" caught in the storm as well?

Mary A. Baker wrote the words to a Hymn in 1874 that captures the sense of panic these disciples were feeling. She penned the following - - -

Master, the tempest is raging!
The billows are tossing high!
The sky is o'ershadow with blackness,
No shelter or help is nigh;
Carest Thou not that we perish?
How canst Thou lie asleep,
When each moment so madly is threatening
A grave in the angry deep?

Master, with anguish of spirit I bow in my grief today;
The depths of my sad heart are troubled
Oh, waken and save, I pray!
Torrents of sin and of anguish
Sweep o'er my sinking soul;
And I perish! I perish! dear Master

Oh, hasten, and take control.

The Refrain bursts out with the words of hope and aspiration. If only Jesus cares enough for us – for me! He could make a considerable difference for us – for me! All one needs is a word from Jesus and all will be well! Does Jesus care? Will Jesus respond? Will He help me? She writes - - -

The winds and the waves shall obey Thy will,
Peace, be still!
Whether the wrath of the storm tossed sea,
Or demons or men, or whatever it be
No waters can swallow the ship where lies
The Master of ocean, and earth, and skies;
They all shall sweetly obey Thy will,
Peace, be still! Peace, be still!
They all shall sweetly obey Thy will,
Peace, peace, be still!

I wonder if it was Peter who called out to Jesus as he posed the question: "Don't You care if we drown (or perish)?" It may have been! Peter was not known for being timid had a way of learning lessons the hard way. The important truth is that he learned. Near the end of his life when the people of his day were facing dire circumstances and persecution, Peter shared with them words that may have been gleaned from his experience on the deck of a storm-tossed boat when a question was screamed out to Jesus – "Don't you care that we are about to drown (perish)?" Note what Peter wrote in I Peter 5:6-7, "Humble yourselves...under God's mighty hand, that he may lift you up in due time. Cast all your anxiety on him because he cares for you." The direction is encompassing, namely, "Cast all..." Some like to control their own destiny and direction, but the wisest decision is to let go of "all" – "cast all your care (anxiety) upon Jesus because He cares for you." Is God serious when He inspired Peter to write them? Are you serious when it comes to implementing these truths in one's daily life? If one is serious about following Christ, there should be no inordinate delays in coming to Him to gain knowledge of His will and provision of His care to sustain His own.

The concern is in terms of whether or not Jesus has become a stranger in His Church and irrelevant in His Creation and world. When I was a child, there was a plaque that was tacked on the trim alongside the dumbwaiter door. It read:

Christ is the head of this house,
The unseen guest at every meal,
The silent listener to every conversation.

The words were significant – World War II was ending and soon, the USA would embark on a "police action" in Korea. Those who arrived at age eighteen were subjected to a Draft Order for the nation. However, It was also a day and time when Jesus Christ was still relevant in our churches, homes and country. The plaque was a constant reminder for us that Jesus Christ cared and is the same yesterday, today and forever. As the years have passed, it seems as though our sense of the centrality of Jesus Christ for our churches, homes and culture has diminished considerably. It is usually in the time of tragedy that one wonders aloud – "What happened to Jesus?" "Where is Jesus when I need Him the most?" It was curious to see on Facebook, after the April 27th, 2011 Tornado swept across the southern states, that someone posed the question: "Where was Jesus when these storms were devastating so many?" Another person speculated and asked: "Is God trying to let us know He is angry with us?" Another question that could be asked is: "Doesn't God have a right to be angry with us when we consider how much we have neglected and ignored Him? Doesn't He have the right to use any means He chooses to gain our attention and to get us to let Him back into our lives?" What if God allowed all of the devastation to remind us of what the disciples may have forgotten when they were in the storm and to ask us – What about the other little boats around you? Have you forgotten all about them? With your building of edifices you say are for Me, have you ignored the "little boats" all around you who may have a different skin color; or a different social status; or a different educational level; or a different cultural style and preference – don't they matter to you? They matter to Me! Why aren't you serious about reaching out to them and their needs? You haven't invited them or sought them out to be part of your church community. Why is that? I was serious when the disciples were instructed through the parable of The Good Samaritan (Luke 10:25-37) of the duty and responsibility to care for the helpless and needy! Why did some pass by – indifferent and uncaring? What would you have done? How serious are you regarding your walk with the Lord?

The questions and suggestions could be many. The issue is that we know what the questions and answers are but we are reluctant to break the mould and to run the risks of being relevant to the whosoever people all around us. There are any number of rural churches that are failing and diminishing in numbers – but – they remain segregated. There are denominational churches in communities that now blend in with other churches in the immediate locale and become Community Churches. Slowly and surely the churches are losing their relevance and distinctiveness - and have become a monument of what once was vibrant and central. Are they relevant in their community regarding the Gospel and Christian life? Relevance is not the issue for them – survival is – they don't want their church to become extinct! It is painful to pass by churches that once were active but are now just a building used occasionally. There are not enough people to gather for a service of worship nor funds enough to maintain the building and property.

The "other little boats" on our horizon – what are we going to do about them? Do we know who are on those boats? Do we care about what needs are present with those on the other little boats? Are they just pesky and an annoyance to us, or do they matter to us because they matter to Jesus? We can't ignore those other little boats – they're out there alongside of us. What would Jesus want us to do about these other little boats on the horizon of our church plants and in our neighbor-hoods? On a much larger scale and in regard to the other little boats, a fascinating column appeared in The Huffington Post on March 23rd, 2011 entitled: "Why Throw Stones At The Crystal Cathedral?" by Tony Campola. He writes:

"As the news of the financial woes of the Crystal Cathedral is heralded across the country and around the world, a host of critical voices have been raised, at times condemning the cost of building the Crystal Cathedral...

"The most common attack has come from those who con-tend that the money spent on building the Crystal Cathedral was not justified. It has been said that the $20 million spent to construct the Crystal Cathedral would have been better spent on such missionary concerns as helping the poor and the oppressed of the world. Before considering the justification for that accusation, however, critics should consider the millions of people who have worshiped at the Crystal Cathedral, Sunday after Sunday, over the years. On a per capita basis, it can easily be proved that less money was spent on this building than has been spent by most congregations on their respective facilities...

"The Crystal Cathedral, in addition to the Sunday morning worship service, also houses one of the largest Hispanic congregations in America. Each Sunday thousands and thousands of Hispanic worshipers gather at the Crystal Cathedral for a special service in their own language. The church also has maintained an extensive ministry to Hispanic youth in its immediate neighborhood. Also, consider that the only Pakistani congregation that I know of in North America (there may be several others), finds a place at the Crystal Cathedral to come together for worship and to organize for Christian service.

"Recently, I went over the list of activities that are part of the ongoing ministries of the Crystal Cathedral. These include classes for those who are learning English as a second language, a host of counseling services and even programs that reach into Los Angeles with help for the homeless. The list of programs sponsored by the Crystal Cathedral is too long to list them all...

"It is quite true that there has been great shrinkage in attendance at the Sunday morning worship services at the Crystal Cathedral. A sanctuary which was once packed with thousands each Sunday now only shows a few hundred at each of its two Sunday morning services, but there are sociological reasons for this decline. The Crystal Cathedral, located in Garden Grove, was once set in the midst of a middle class, Anglo-Saxon, Protestant community from which it received great support. This community has changed, however, and today Garden Grove is a predominantly Hispanic neighborhood. Consequently, the Crystal Cathedral has lost a large part of its congregation...because, like many churches, the community that it once served has changed. The good news is that the Crystal Cathedral responded by embracing neighboring Hispanic people with an array of specialized, needed ministries. Sadly, those ministries have not provided much income -- certainly not enough to keep the Crystal Cathedral out of bankruptcy..."

While Tony Campolo has made some interesting observations, it is not the design or intent of this Book or Chapter to commend, condone or condemn the ministry of the Crystal Cathedral. There is much about the Philosophy of Ministry and Theology there that could be examined and scrutinized, but that will have to wait for another time and another book. At the very least, they have tried to adapt to the changing demographic in which they are located. The point being made here is to point out the truth and fact of life is that communities and demographics do change. Schools and Local Stores relocate to the newer population centers or cease to exist. The children who grew up in the community have sought employment and made their homes elsewhere. Churches often relocate to where "their people" are and inner cities become abandoned – leaving many empty stores and homes that are no longer maintained. It would be impossible to relocate the Crystal Cathedral – it must either adapt or cease to exist. In some places, these inner cities are identified as ghettoes. Just another little boat on the horizon of our times and world. One large Church found itself in a changing demographic and made a decision not to minister to the people of color that surrounded their "church" facility – even though they maintained a large missionary budget to support those who went to other countries in our world and who were ministering to people of color. From its position of influence, it found that the attendance and financial support was declining – and – it soon came to the point where it no longer exists. The property was purchased by a group that was neither fearful nor hesitant to promote and engage in an integrated ministry – and today – in that very same location – it is thriving in its ministry. It would be of great value if there was a way to communicate a vision of ministry opportunity so that the other little boats do not get left-behind to capsize in the troubled sea.

There are words to a Christian song written by Ross H. Minkler based upon Proverbs 29:18, "Where there is no vision the people cast off restraint (and perish)…" Some of what Minkler wrote is - - -

Lord, give me a vision, oh, help me to see
The needs all around me; souls dying for Thee;
Oh, make me a blessing, as onward I go,
By telling the story, that others may know.

Lord, give me a vision, oh, help me to see
Some neighbor today, Lord, and bring him to Thee,
That on that glad morning, some soul there may say,
The prayers of God's children have shown me the way.

It is vital for the one seeking to show another the right way that he has the discernment to adequately accomplish that goal and task. Henry Blackaby makes the statement in his book on Leadership: "If you can't see where you are going you are unlikely to get there. If you don't get there no one you are leading will either." I often wonder if the young Pastor who suffers from disillusionment in ministry began his ministry with all the positive aspirations and hopes. His dreams and goals were lofty – his vision and ideals were commendable. One day along the way he began to realize that even though his dreams and goals were lofty – and right – the people did not respond to him or them. He realized that his vision and ideals, while commendable, were not being fully embraced by the people who he believed he was called to lead – and wanted to lead. He began to feel that he was out front leading the charge but when he turned around and looked – no one was following. How sad and discouraging, how disappointing – what a disillusionment. He began to think he was a failure – and so – laid down his sword and quit. He had forgotten the words of Scripture in Galatians 6:9-10, "And let us not grow weary of doing good, for in due season we will reap, if we do not give up. So then, as we have opportunity, let us do good to everyone, and especially to those who are of the household of faith." Additionally, he had forgotten the words of perspective and determination written by The Apostle Paul in II Corinthians 4:7-10, "But we have this treasure in jars of clay, to show that the surpassing power belongs to God and not to us. We are afflicted in every way, but not crushed; perplexed, but not driven to despair; persecuted, but not forsaken; struck down, but not destroyed; always carrying in the body the death of Jesus, so that the life of Jesus may also be manifested in our bodies."

These excellent words of encouragement from God's Word are good and helpful – but – too easily forgotten when it comes to a lonely pastoral ministry – or – one of the other little boats bobbing on the stormy waves and very near to sinking. Sometimes – many times – it is the little boat that needs us the most and will respond to us most readily. Let us not grow weary! On the horizon is the King of Glory waiting to return to claim His bride and take us home to be with Him forevermore. Let us reflect His love to all the other little boats we see and with whom we have contact. God is absolutely serious about His direction and His care! Are you completely serious about your commitment to follow Him?

May God richly bless you as you serve Him!

QUESTIONS FOR THOUGHT AND APPLICATION

Chapter Two continues with thoughts regarding Natural Disasters and desperate situations that one can encounter. It seems as though, the greater the catastrophe, the greater the awareness by others becomes. Since the original writing of this Book, two different and horrific incidents occurred in the Northeastern United States. First was the widespread impact of Hurricane Sandy in New Jersey, New York and Connecticut with considerable destruction, loss of services – electricity, absence of pure drinking water, as well as irreplaceable personal losses. Second was the senseless rampage by a young man who entered an elementary school in Newtown, Connecticut – shooting and killing twenty young children and six adults. In moments of panic and fear, one often heard (and hears) the expression: "Oh, my God!"

1.   When one is heard to cry out in despair or fear – "Oh, my God" – is that an earnest effort to Take A Serious God Seriously, or is it a linguistic phenomenon that is common in this culture? Does that expression and use of "God" qualify as taking His name in vain?

2.   Overall, does the culture/society view "God" as One Who is relevant or irrelevant? Why do you think so?

3.   If you were asked to establish a viable and relevant strategy for advancing the cause of Christ in your community and church, what would the first three priorities be?

4.   If Jesus was inhabiting your community today, and He said to the short-sighted and/or ineffective church members the words recorded in John 4:28-36 (NKJV), "Do you not say, 'There

are still four months and then comes the harvest'? Behold, I say to you, Lift up your eyes and Look at the fields, for they are already white (ripe) for harvest..." who would He be seeing and to whom would He be referring?

- Would they be people one would naturally "like"?
- Would they be people with whom we have "socialized" in public and private life?
- Would they be people who would ordinarily want to affiliate with us in any capacity?
- To whom is Jesus referring when He says: "...Look at the fields...they are already white (ripe) for harvest"?

5.   If different ethnic people were being reached and desired to become part of the spiritual community that is sometimes referred to as "our church", would we welcome them, or if they persisted in attending, would we leave "our church"? Why?

6.   When Jesus Christ used the word "all", did He mean that we could substitute the word "some" as an accommodation for our culture or ethnic orientation?

7.   Is the Gospel of Jesus Christ intended to be "inclusive" or "exclusive"? Why?

Jesus came and stood in the midst, and said to them, "Peace be with you."... Jesus said to them again, "Peace to you! As the Father has sent Me, I also send you."
                                             John 20:19-21 (NKJV – Selected)

Functional or Failing Foundations

Isaiah 24:11-19 speaks of a moment when the Foundations of the Universe will be impacted. It speaks of a cataclysmic event that will affect all nations and all people. Isaiah writes: "The earth is violently broken, The earth is split open, The earth is shaken exceedingly. The earth shall reel to and fro like a drunkard, And shall totter like a hut; Its transgression shall be heavy upon it, And it will fall, and not rise again. It shall come to pass in that day That the Lord will punish on high the host of exalted ones, And on the earth the kings of the earth. They will be gathered together, As prisoners are gathered in the pit, And will be shut up in the prison; After many days they will be punished. Then the moon will be disgraced And the sun ashamed; For the Lord of hosts will reign On Mount Zion and in Jerusalem And before His elders, gloriously."

In World War II, August 1945, Japan was the first nation that became the target of nuclear warfare, namely, Atomic Bombs. A uranium bomb, was dropped from the Enola Gay over Hiroshima at 8:15 a.m. on August 6, 1945. One minute later, 66,000 people were dead and 69,000 injured from the 10-kiloton atomic explosion. Nagasaki was attacked three days later by a plutonium bomb responsible for 39,000 deaths and 25,000 injuries. Quickly, Japan decided to surrender and all hostilities were brought to a halt. These bombings gained the attention of a determined enemy. The enemy realized that the Allied Forces were serious regarding victory and that they had no defense against the nuclear weapons. Surrender became a life and death matter – to refuse was to be inflicted with further destruction – it was that serious display or power and determinations that brought the enemy to ponder the serious consideration, namely, to surrender!

Jesus spoke about the Values and Foundations with those who gathered around him. He did so as He gave The Sermon on the Mount that spoke of the choices and options one has and makes in life. His words about Foundations are in Matthew 7:24-29 - "Therefore whoever hears these sayings of Mine, and does them, I will liken him to a wise man who built his house on the rock: and the rain descended, the floods came, and the winds blew and beat on that house; and it did not fall, for it was founded on the rock. But everyone who hears these sayings of Mine, and does not do them, will be like a foolish man who built his house on the sand: and the rain descended, the floods came, and the winds blew and beat on that house; and it fell. And great was its fall. And so it was, when Jesus had ended these sayings, that the people were astonished at His teaching, for He taught them as one having authority, and not as the scribes."

The choice seems very obvious: The Wise Man chooses the Rock for his structural foundation. The Foolish Man chooses the Sand for his structural foundation. The reasons that may have been in the mind of The Foolish Man may have been cost containment and more immediate use for the structure built. It is also possible that he had no experience in the pros and cons of structures and their foundations.

In modern architecture, that is 20th and 21st Century, considerable emphasis is placed upon the principle of Form and Function as it relates to a particular building. The American architect, Louis Sullivan, coined the phrase in 1896 when he wrote an article on: "The Tall Office Building Is Artistically

Considered." It was in that article that Sullivan actually said 'form ever follows function', but the simpler and less emphatic phrase is the one usually remembered. For Sullivan this was distilled wisdom, an aesthetic credo, the single "rule that shall permit of no exception". The full quote is thus: "It is the pervading law of all things organic and inorganic; Of all things physical and metaphysical; Of all things human and all things super-human; Of all true manifestations of the head, of the heart, of the soul; That the life is recognizable in its expression; That form ever follows function. This is the law." While it is not stated in Sullivan's Credo, the necessary and basic consideration would follow that the taller the building the deeper the foundation.

When architectural plans were made for the building of the Empire State Building, there had to be consideration for the stability of the structure. After careful planning, the outcome was a structure that is "...1,453 feet 8 and 9/16th inches tall from street level to its highest point -- a lightning rod. This is on top of the foundation of bedrock which rests 55 feet below ground." The building was completed in 1931 and continues to this day in its place of recognition and dominance in the Skyline of the City. Part of the reason is that importance was placed upon the Foundation, as well as on the Form and Function of the structure.

Foundations in the erection of Buildings are vital and to be subject to serious calculations. However, in Spiritual Matters, the foundations are much more vital. God is serious about His proclamations, desires, and directives. If one chooses to be less than serious regarding spiritual matters, there will be a devastating result. The Psalmist raised an important thought that he shared in Psalm 11:2-3, "The wicked bend their bow, They make ready their arrow on the string, That they may shoot secretly at the upright in heart. If the foundations are destroyed, What can the righteous do?"

He is speaking of spiritual warfare and the battle for the souls of men. It is facing the reality of the conflict between the forces of evil against the righteous. It ponders the plight of the righteous and their alternative when he asks: "What can the righteous do?" That question is expressed in greater detail in Psalm 74:4-9 - "Your enemies roar in the midst of Your meeting place; They set up their banners for signs. They seem like men who lift up Axes among the thick trees. And now they break down its carved work, all at once, With axes and hammers. They have set fire to Your sanctuary; They have defiled the dwelling place of Your name to the ground. They said in their hearts, Let us destroy them altogether They have burned up all the meeting places of God in the land. We do not see our signs; There is no longer any prophet; Nor is there any among us who knows how long." This is a serious attempt to war against The God of Heaven and His people who continue to reside upon Earth.

The Psalmist is describing the desecration and destruction of everything that had been traditionally deemed secure. The Message paraphrase states it: "While your people were at worship, your enemies barged in, brawling and scrawling graffiti. They set fire to the porch; axes swinging, they chopped up the woodwork, Beat down the doors with sledgehammers, then split them into kindling. They burned your holy place to the ground, violated the place of worship. They said to themselves, We'll wipe them all out, and burned down all the places of worship. There's not a sign or symbol of God in sight, nor anyone to speak in his name, no one who knows what's going on." A question not asked here deals with the expression and use of the term "worship." Jesus was serious when He uttered – John 4:22-24 – "You worship what you do not know; we worship what we know, for salvation is from the Jews. But the hour is coming, and is now here, when the true worshipers will worship the Father in spirit and truth, for the Father is seeking such people to worship him. God is spirit, and those who worship him must worship in spirit and truth." The question God might ask in this situation is simply: "What Worship is being offered to Him? Do you call what you are doing "Worship" that I want and that honors Me? Why do you merely go through religious motions and embrace only your traditions and rituals – why aren't you embracing Me in your worship ceremony?" Why aren't you as serious about regular worship as I am?

On the subject of Foundations, In Preaching Today Sermons, Ravi Zacharias shares these thoughts on Psalm 74 - "The Topic: What happens to our culture as the foundations of faith are abandoned? The Big Idea: Although the cultural revolution has abandoned the fundamental foundations of faith, restoration is possible if Christians will light the way.

(1) We are thrust into a humanistic world view, and we wonder how it happened.

(2) A cultural revolution is under way, and we must respond.

(3) As we come unhinged from our Creator, our culture's foundations are being destroyed

(4) The antagonism against things spiritual is real.

(5) The revolution strikes at the jugular of every institution in the land.

(6) God created us to be accountable for our actions, but that has been lost.

(7) By losing accountability, we've eradicated conscience. (8) God gave us charity, but that has been lost. We have lost the idea of beneficence."

These are very timely, as well as timeless, considerations for such a time as this. The bigger question becomes – "What can and should one do about it? Where can one begin?" The Psalmist asked the question: "If the foundations are destroyed, What can the righteous do?" The Message renders Psalm 11:3, "The bottom's dropped out of the country; good people don't have a chance!" What should you seriously consider doing? Where will you begin? What will you do?

In starting with the basics – foundation truths – the idea is to keep it as simple as possible. The words of the Apostle Paul in I Corinthians 2:2-5 are clearly in view: "For I resolved to know nothing while I was with you except Jesus Christ and him crucified. I came to you in weakness and fear, and with much trembling. My message and my preaching were not with wise and persuasive words, but with a demonstration of the Spirit's power, so that your faith might not rest on men's wisdom, but on God's power." This is the Foundation upon which these chapters are being built. They will focus on the Triune God and the Eternal Purpose of Redemption in, through and by Jesus Christ. It begins with the basic presupposition/fact that The Eternal God is real and has always existed, and that He has spoken and revealed Himself in His Word and in His Son. This conviction is based upon the following:

(1) Genesis 1:1 - In the beginning – GOD;

(2) John 1:1-2 - In the beginning was The WORD, and The WORD was with GOD , and The WORD was God. He was in the beginning with GOD.

(3) The Foundational Thought: God always was and always will be – He Alone is Eternal.

To develop this foundation and structure for your faith, the broad concept and outline of the Ordo Salutis (The Order of Salvation) will be followed. In the book: "Theological Terms In Laymen's Language" by Martin Murphy, he defines Ordo Salutis in this way: "It refers to the logical order of the causes and effects which produce salvation. The different aspects to the ordo salutis are election, calling, regeneration, conversion (including repentance and faith), justification, adoption, sanctification, and glorification." Another publication, Redemption Accomplished and Applied by John Murray gives an expanded study on the subject: The Ordo Salutis.

A clear distinction must be made that the order is Logical – not necessarily Sequential. Some aspects of the Order occur simultaneously – but – all are occurring within God's plan and purpose – the Eternal Will of God. A Key Passage that will substantiate many of the points made in the following chapters is Ephesians 1:4-11 – " Praise be to the God and Father of our Lord Jesus Christ, who has blessed us in the heavenly realms with every spiritual blessing in Christ. For he chose us in him before the creation of the world to be holy and blameless in his sight. In love he predestined us to be adopted as his sons through Jesus Christ, in accordance with his pleasure and will-- to the praise of his glorious grace, which he has freely given us in the One he loves. In him we have redemption through his blood, the forgiveness of sins, in accordance with the riches of God's grace that he lavished on us with all wisdom and understanding. And he made known to us the mystery of his will according to his good pleasure, which he purposed in Christ, to be put into effect when the times will have reached their fulfillment--to bring all things in heaven and on earth together under one head, even Christ. In him we were also chosen, having been predestined according to the plan of him who works out everything in conformity with the purpose of his will..."

Another passage is in Acts 2:22-36, Peter's sermon on The Day of Pentecost after Jesus had ascended into Heaven - "...Jesus of Nazareth, a man attested to you by God with mighty works and wonders and signs that God did through him in your midst, as you yourselves know -- this Jesus, delivered up according to the definite plan and fore-knowledge of God, you crucified and killed by the hands of lawless men. God raised him up, loosing the pangs of death, because it was not possible for him to be held by it...This Jesus God raised up, and of that we all are witnesses. Being therefore exalted at the right hand of God, and having received from the Father the promise of the Holy Spirit, he has poured out this that you yourselves are seeing and hearing...Let all the house of Israel therefore know for certain that God has made him both Lord and Christ, this Jesus whom you crucified." At the very least, Peter is address-ing (a) predestination – "according to the definite plan and foreknowledge of God; (b) Christ's crucifixion; (c) Christ's resurrection; (d) Christ's exaltation and glorification.

One other passage that is part of the background for these chapters is: Romans 8:28-30, "And we know that for those who love God all things work together for good, for those who are called according to his purpose. For those whom he foreknew he also predestined to be conformed to the image of his Son, in order that he might be the firstborn among many brothers. And those whom he predestined he also called, and those whom he

called he also justified, and those whom he justified he also glorified." The passage indicates:
(a) effectual calling – called according to His purpose
(b) predestined to be conformed to the image of His Son
(c) those predestined – He called, He justified, He glorified.
These are some of the basics that should serve as the Foundation for your Faith. These things represent the bedrock rather than the sand. These things are the diet of meat/solid food rather than one of milk.

In a warning against apostasy and an observation regarding where many professing Christians are found, Hebrews 5:12-14 states: "For though by this time you ought to be teachers, you need someone to teach you again the basic principles of the oracles of God. You need milk, not solid food, for everyone who lives on milk is unskilled in the word of righteousness, since he is a child. But solid food is for the mature, for those who have their powers of discernment trained by constant practice to distinguish good from evil." The goal and aim is to go on to maturity in the Word – the solid food that will result in spiritual maturity.

There is an old Hymn that was written before 1800 that places great emphasis upon the firm foundation upon which one is to build his/her faith.

How firm a foundation, ye saints of the Lord,
Is laid for your faith in His excellent Word!
What more can He say than to you He hath said,
You, who unto Jesus for refuge have fled?

Fear not, I am with thee, O be not dismayed,
For I am thy God and will still give thee aid;

I'll strengthen and help thee, and cause thee to stand
Upheld by My righteous, omnipotent hand.

When through fiery trials thy pathways shall lie,
My grace, all sufficient, shall be thy supply;
The flame shall not hurt thee; I only design
Thy dross to consume, and thy gold to refine.

The soul that on Jesus has leaned for repose,
I will not, I will not desert to its foes;
That soul, though all hell should endeavor to shake,
I'll never, no never, no never forsake.

A Hymn that expresses similar thoughts was penned in the mid-1800s and expresses:

The Church's one foundation Is Jesus Christ her Lord,
She is His new creation By water and the Word.
From heaven He came and sought her
To be His holy bride;
With His own blood He bought her And for her life He died.

'Mid toil and tribulation, And tumult of her war,
She waits the consummation Of peace forevermore;
Till, with the vision glorious, Her longing eyes are blest,
And the great Church victorious Shall be the Church at rest.

QUESTIONS FOR THOUGHT AND APPLICATION

Paul writes about the different possibilities in terms of what can be chosen and used for a foundation in one's life. Read – I Corinthians 3:11-15...

For no other foundation can anyone lay than that which is laid, which is Jesus Christ. Now if anyone builds on this foundation with gold, silver, precious stones, wood, hay, straw, each one's work will become clear; for the Day will declare it, because it will be revealed by fire; and the fire will test each one's work, of what sort it is. If anyone's work which he has built on it endures, he will receive a reward. If anyone's work is burned, he will suffer loss; but he himself will be saved, yet so as through fire.

1. What are the two foundations Paul mentions?

2. What would be the best and wisest choice for a foundation?

3. In Paul's illustration, what is the test that will determine whether or not one's choice was the correct one?

4. Jesus also discusses foundations and the available choices in Matthew 7:24-27.
What are the two foundations Jesus mentions?

What would be the best choice for a foundation? Is this your current reality?

In Jesus' illustration, what is the test that will determine whether or not ones choice was the correct one?

5. Based on these two illustrations, what is in the balance of the choice one makes?

6. Why is the choice significant and important?

7. Do you believe God is serious about all that He has revealed in His Word?

8. What is the intention of God's Revelation?

9. Could it be that He wants one to know what he/she is to believe concerning God, and what duty He requires of mankind?

10. Is He serious about this reality?

11. Are you as serious about it as He is? Is it an imposition for one to be as serious as God is about this foundational reality?

12. Ideally and positionally, where would you desire to be in your walk with the Lord?

When we walk with the Lord in the light of His Word,
 What a glory He sheds on our way!
 While we do His good will, He abides with us still,
 And with all who will trust and obey.

Refrain

Trust and obey, for there's no other way
 To be happy in Jesus, but to trust and obey.

An Eroding Standard

In the twenty-first century, there is a consistent trend unfolding in terms of the educational values and achievement level of children in Grades One through Twelve. In a study done and released under the title of: "International Test Scores - Poor U.S. Test Results Tied To Weak Curriculum" it has been found that students in the American Educational System are not fairing too well. The study was done within a targeted area with the following parameters: "Math and Science offer the only common basis for comparing American schools to the rest of the world. Other subjects vary from one country to another. Results of the Third International Mathematics and Science Study (TIMSS) involving a half-million students in 41 countries are authoritative. Oversight groups included not only the world's leading experts on comparative studies of education systems, but also experts in assessment design and statistical analysis." The results of the study reveal that at Grade Level 4 – the United States ranks Number 12 (out of 26 Nations scored); at Grade Level 8 – the United States ranks Number 28 (out of 41 Nations scored); and at Grade Level 12 – the United States ranks Number 19 (out of 21 Nations scored). The conclusions drawn by some of those involved in the Test Score Study is summarized in their statement titled: "Causes for Failure."

Note some of their conclusions: "One would think that with our vastly superior resources and the level of education spending which far exceeds these competitors we would outperform nearly everyone - not so... The actual cause for the failures appears to be weak math and science curricula in U.S. middle schools. A more insightful explanation was...proffered by Jean

McLaughlin, president of Barry University who said: The public schools lack focus; instead of concentrating on education, they dabble in social re-engineering. That assessment was confirmed by the superintendent of the country's fourth largest school district in Miami-Dade, Florida who said: Half our job is education, and the other half is social work. Downward sloping performance confirms John Taylor Gatto's thesis in his book "Dumbing Us Down."

Does the secular educational trends impact the spiritual climate and thinking in a similar way? If the above trends are present in the public domain of education at the grassroots level, is there a similar trend in religion and the level of Biblical knowledge, discernment and application in what is known as "The Church" in contemporary society? Is there the possibility of an ongoing "dumbing-down" within certain venues of the so-called "Christian Church"? A report was released some time ago by George Barna [2005] entitled "Religious & Church Trends." In that article, George Barna indicated that his studies have found particular trends and deficiencies within churches in the United States. He reports: There are factors "indicative of the reshaping of the church in the U.S. The first of those patterns has to do with the priorities embraced by church leaders. He noted that most local churches essentially ignore three critical spiritual dimensions: (a) ministry to children, (b) ministry to families, and (c) the ministry of prayer. The statistics showed that less than one out of every five Protestant churches deem ministry to families or to children to be among the top priorities of the church. Prayer...is labeled one of the top priorities by less than one out of every 25 churches!

"A second church-related trend indicates congregations are rapidly incorporating new technologies into their activities, such as, big-screen projection systems (now used by almost two-thirds of all Protestant churches), Web sites (57%) and e-mail blasts to congregants (56%)." The rationale is: "These are tools that draw people to church events, that help churches communicate more effectively, and that have the capacity to provide a more compelling and memorable experience...The integration of these applications into the church's normal process also conveys an image of cultural sensitivity and relevance to those who are trying to determine if the church has something valid to offer."

"A third church-related trend...among the many changes reshaping the church world, one of the most invisible, yet significant, is the changing of the guard among the leaders of the leaders. Referring to the individuals whom the media and general public, as well as pastors, perceive to be the leading spokespersons for the Christian Church in the U.S. a study showing that the leading representatives of the Christian faith now (2011) include names like Rick Warren, T.D. Jakes and Joel Osteen. In the past three decades, the representatives included Billy Graham, Adrian Rogers, Jerry Falwell, John MacArthur, Pat Robertson, Robert Schuller, D. James Kennedy and Charles Stanley. He also pointed out that the different faith communities in the nation — that is, mainline, charismatic, evangelical, ethnic — each have their own go-to people, which he sees as being symptomatic of the fragmented nature of the Christian Church in the United States."

If George Barna is correct in his findings, the pattern of the secular state has also infiltrated the "Christian church" to a much larger degree than most are willing to admit. It would behoove the church at large to examine its foundational principles and core beliefs to determine whether or not they are consistent with God's Word and God's Will for His Church and His People. If a particular church has allowed itself to succumb to "the least common denominator" approach and to assume the posture of being "all things to all men", then the individual must determine if there is anything worthwhile and edifying in the ministry that has compromised its values. The question is, should a committed Christian who is yielded to the Lord Jesus Christ remain in a ministry that has allowed for a diminished and eroding standard of belief and practice?

In Literature, most have read or heard the reading of Hamlet's Soliloquy by William Shakespeare. The opening words are: "To be, or not to be: that is the question: Whether 'tis nobler in the mind to suffer The slings and arrows of outrageous fortune, Or to take arms against a sea of troubles, And by opposing end them?" The phrase to single out is: "To be, or not to be; that is the question." A related question is: What are we supposed to be, and conversely, what are we supposed not to be…? This is the question that must be addressed, pondered, studied and resolved by the "Christian Church" in today's world. In keeping with this approach to the Church in the 21st Century, a similar thought was shared In a Blog Post on the webpage of UB-Friends.org. The entry from March 2011 followed the idea of "to be or not to be" and expressed it as: "To Stay or Not To Stay?" The intent of the Blog is to get people to face and consider the reality of the infusion of liberal teaching and practices into a historic and/or evangelical community of believers. This material comes from the question that Dr. D. Martyn Lloyd-Jones addressed in 1966 at the National Assembly of Evangelicals conference in England. In the course of his presentation, some of what he said and suggested was in response to some concerns regarding: When is it a good idea to stay in a church or para-church ministry, and when is it better to leave? Lloyd-Jones was a very respected evangelical leader, and he used this opportunity to implore evangelicals to leave the Church of England because it was tolerating theologically liberal people and ideas in its ranks. He expanded his application so it would address another concern, namely, what if a church teaches essentially correct doctrine but its overall systematic practices go against its teaching? Lloyd-Jones had an issue with the Anglican Church because, while their doctrinal statement was basically solid, according to him, its practices across the board over time were not and so he advocated separation in that case..."

What applications can be drawn from either question – (a) to be or not to be, or (b) to stay or not to stay? What is the standard and what is the safeguard that can prevent a church body from diminishing and/or eroding the foundational beliefs and core values that have been embraced by earlier generations? Should we be concerned and should we address these concerns with practical and valid alternatives for the present trends? Where does one begin and what should one do to preserve faithfulness to God's Standard and commitment to His values? We can get a hint from some concluding remarks and conclusions drawn by those who conducted the study on the International Test Score. Their summary touches upon three basic and necessary areas: (1) Curricula; (2) Teachers; and (3) Textbooks. A summary of their statement is the following:

"(1) Curricula - The biggest deficits are found at the middle school level. In middle school, most countries shift curricula from basic arithmetic and elementary science in the direction of chemistry, physics, algebra and geometry. Even poor countries generally teach a half-year of algebra and a half-year of geometry to every eighth-grader. In U.S. middle schools, however, most students continue to review arithmetic. And they are more likely to study earth science and life science than physics or chemistry.

"(2) Teachers - Among teachers of high school biology and life sciences classes, approximately 31 percent of them do not have at least a minor in biology. Among high school physical science teachers, over half, 55 percent, do not have at least a minor in any of the physical sciences. Again, we might question the focus of the teachers on social re-engineering instead of subject areas.

"(3) Textbooks - U.S. textbooks treat topics with a "mile-wide, inch-deep" approach, Schmidt said. A typical U.S. eighth-grade math textbook deals with about 35 topics. By comparison, a Japanese or German math textbook for that age would have only five or six topics. Comparisons done elsewhere between French and American math books show more innovative approaches to finding, for instance, the volume of a pyramid. Fractions don't lend themselves to computerization, so they're relegated to an importance slightly above Roman numerals. Calculators are here to stay, so kids breeze through long division. They concentrate on how to use math rather than how to do math, and with less entanglement in social philosophy.

"American Education Is Not World Class - The schools systematically let kids down. By Grade 4, American students only score in the middle of 26 countries reported. By Grade 8 they are in the bottom third, and at the finish line, where it really counts, we're near dead last. Its even worse when you notice that some of the superior countries in Grade 8 (especially the

Asians) were not included in published 12th Grade results. They do not need 12 Grades."

These findings should not only strike us as being unacceptable and exceedingly sad, but also trending toward a great disaster for the future of the children of this country and the nation as it seeks to maintain a position of significance in this highly competitive world. In a far more significant and important area, namely, the "Christian" community, have these same trends have found entrance and they are adversely impacting the "church" as a whole? Is the "Christian church" striving towards achievement and excellence or is it content to move sideways and "mark-time" at the present levels? The question posed in Psalm 11:3 is both a haunting and compelling one: "...if the foundations are destroyed, what can the righteous do?" If all of what should be dear to us is being diminished and eroded before our eyes, should we remain silent and merely accept things as they are and never utter a word of protest and alternative?

If one is going to enter the arena and endeavor to make a difference, one ought to be prepared adequately to address the issues of concern. One must not be disillusioned. Upon entering the arena, there will be opposition – strong and fierce. There are hazards and dangers of all sorts. It is good to recall the words spoken by Theodore Roosevelt in a Speech at the Sorbonne, Paris, April 23, 1910, Citizenship In A Republic:

"It is not the critic who counts: not the man who points out how the strong man stumbles or where the doer of deeds could have done better. The credit belongs to the man who is actually in the arena, whose face is marred by dust and sweat and blood, who strives valiantly, who errs and comes up short again and again, because there is no effort without error or shortcoming, but who knows the great enthusiasms, the great devotions, who spends himself for a worthy cause; who, at the best, knows, in the end, the triumph of high achievement, and who, at the worst, if he fails, at least he fails while daring greatly, so that his place shall never be with those cold and timid souls who knew neither victory nor defeat."

The responsibility is that one must know all about the foundation, determining and making certain that it is sound, and to begin building on it. This must be done without compromise. Will there be hindrances? Yes! Will there be opposition? Yes! Can the battle be fierce? Yes! Those who should be building along with you on the solid foundation are among those who wittingly or unwittingly have contributed to it being diminished and eroded. They are the ones who have compromised and who will not change from that position because of their desire for broad acceptance and gaining approval by the secular community. They may admire you for your courage and willingness to "earnestly contend for the faith" as you believe it – but – they will not identify with your cause or stand with you as they should.

There is a descriptive statement made in the Book of Jude, The Message paraphrase – especially verses 3-4: "Dear friends, I've dropped everything to write you about this life of salvation that we have in common. I have to write insisting - begging! - that you fight with everything you have in you for this faith entrusted to us as a gift to guard and cherish. What has happened is that some people have infiltrated our ranks (our Scriptures warned us this would happen), who beneath their pious skin are shameless scoundrels. Their design is to replace the sheer grace of our God with sheer license - which means doing away with Jesus Christ, our one and only Master...." The gradualism that has occurred has regrettably allowed too many to become nonchalant and drowsy, whereas they need to be alert and vigilant. The "scoundrels" represent one who is known for his subtlety. This is a reason why Paul wrote in II Corinthians 2:11, "...so that we would not be outwitted by Satan; for we are not ignorant of his designs (schemes)." The Message renders the verse: "After all, we don't want to unwittingly give Satan an opening for yet more mischief - we're not oblivious to his sly ways!"

As one becomes engaged in the ongoing battle to adhere to the foundational principles and standards, there is another striking passage in Proverbs 6:12-19 that gives indication of why there is deterioration of quality within the church and why there is presence of the diminishing and eroding of the standards and foundations. The verses state: "A worthless person, a wicked man, goes about with crooked speech, winks with his eyes, signals with his feet, points with his finger, with perverted heart devises evil, continually sowing discord; therefore calamity will come upon him suddenly; in a moment he will be broken beyond healing. There are six things that the Lord hates, seven that are an abomination to him: haughty eyes, a lying tongue, and hands that shed innocent blood, a heart that devises wicked plans, feet that make haste to run to evil, a false witness who breathes out lies, and one who sows discord among brothers."

Think of these words in terms of how the local church is governed and those who have been selected to do that governing. Have you ever observed this behavior described in Proverbs 6 among those who are touted to be church leaders? Have you ever wondered how certain individuals were elevated to a position of a "church leader"? Is there any criteria by which one should be measured to determine whether or not this is God's man for the task?

A starting place to ascertain a minimum standard for the one chosen to be a leader is given in Acts 6:1-7. It should be noted that the suggestion of the text is that these men were being selected of a menial task – but – that did not minimize the type man to be chosen to do that task. This was to be the solid foundation and the uncompromised foundation as the Church began and developed. The text states: "Now in these days when the disciples were increasing in number, a complaint by the Hellenists arose against the Hebrews because their widows were being neglected in the daily distribution. And the twelve summoned the full number of the disciples and said: It is not right that we should give up preaching the word of God to serve tables. Therefore, brothers, pick out from among you seven men of good repute, full of the Spirit and of wisdom, whom we will appoint to this duty. But we will devote our-selves to prayer and to the ministry of the word. And what they said pleased the whole gathering, and they chose Stephen, a man full of faith and of the Holy Spirit...These they set before the apostles, and they prayed and laid their hands on them. And the word of God continued to increase, and the number of the disciples multiplied greatly in Jerusalem, and a great many of the priests became obedient to the faith."

The basic requirement was to chose those who were "men of good repute, full of the Spirit and of wisdom..." There is the minimum standard – (a) men of good reputation; (b) men full of the Holy Spirit, and (c) men of wisdom (spiritual knowledge and discernment). If the believers were obedient in this impor-tant area, the result will be "...the word of God continued to increase, and the number of the disciples multiplied greatly..."

There is no mystery regarding what God wants as His man for His tasks whether they be menial or the most noble.

As the Church grew, multiplied and expanded, the same occurred with the minimum requirement. It was refined, clarified and amplified. Additional stipulations were attached and adherence to them was expected – free from any change, alteration or modification. Church Leadership was defined and organized in two primary areas: Overseer (Elder) and Deacon. For the Overseer, the minimum requirement was amplified and the stipulations clarified. In I Timothy 3:1-7, the basics and qualifications are given: "The saying is trustworthy: If anyone aspires to the office of overseer, he desires a noble task. Therefore an overseer must be above reproach, the husband of one wife, sober-minded, self-controlled, respectable, hospitable, able to teach, not a drunkard, not violent but gentle, not quarrelsome, not a lover of money. He must manage his own household well, with all dignity keeping his children submissive, for if someone does not know how to manage his own household, how will he care for God's church? He must not be a recent convert, or he may become puffed up with conceit and fall into the condemnation of the devil. Moreover, he must be well thought of by outsiders, so that he may not fall into disgrace, into a snare of the devil." This must be the standard followed and the measurement of the man who would be elevated to the noble task ministry of an Overseer. It must also be noted that this is God's requirement – God's standard. Obviously, it must be adhered to free of any compromise or alteration. If the Church can learn to function in God's Church in God's Way then the Church can expect and receive God's Blessing.

The minimum requirement and standard for the Deacon, the one who will serve in some of the menial and maintenance task, was also amplified and stated in I Timothy 3:8-13, "Deacons likewise must be dignified, not double-tongued, not addicted to much wine, not greedy for dishonest gain. They must hold the mystery of the faith with a clear conscience. And let them also be tested first; then let them serve as deacons if they prove themselves blameless. Their wives likewise must be dignified, not slanderers, but sober-minded, faithful in all things. Let deacons each be the husband of one wife, managing their children and their own households well. For those who serve well as deacons gain a good standing for themselves and also great confidence in the faith that is in Christ Jesus." Another Chapter will deal with these requirements and how a candidate for either the office of Overseer (Elder) or Deacon should be instructed, qualified and approved for these special areas of ministry for the Lord Jesus Christ. A Contemporary Worship Chorus can serve well as the prayer for any man being considered for the Church Ministry of an Overseer (Elder) or a Deacon. The words are:

Make me a servant, humble and meek
Lord, let me lift up, those who are weak.
And may the prayer of my heart always be;
Make me a servant, make me a servant,
Make me a servant, today.

The Church should expect nothing less than a man with a servant's heart. God will not honor or bless the one who is ego-driven or proud. We need to seek the heart of our Master – the Lord Jesus Christ – and emulate His life and Character. We get a glimpse of it in Philippians 2:5-8, "...Have this mind among yourselves, which is yours in Christ Jesus, Who, though he was in the form of God, did not count equality with God a thing to be grasped, but made himself nothing, taking the form of a servant, being born in the likeness of men. And being found in human form, he humbled himself by becoming obedient..." We look at two phrases where it is said: "He made Himself nothing...He humbled Himself by becoming obedient..." and ask ourselves – Can that be said about me? Is that my character? Is that how I will serve my Savior and Master? Don't shrink back from Him or what He modeled for us. Let your prayer be: Lord – make me a servant – grant me a heart like Yours. I want to be Your servant! I want to represent you before the world with humility and meekness. I want to be usable and useful for You and Your Kingdom. This represents Taking A Serious God Seriously.

In a Contemporary Worship Chorus, Words and Music by Terrye Coelho, is a simple and basic expression of Worship and Commitment. May this by your song – our song -of worship and commitment to our Lord.

Father, I adore You Lay my life before You
How I love You!

Jesus, I adore You Lay my life before You
How I love You!

Spirit I adore You Lay my life before You
How I love You - How I love You!

QUESTIONS FOR THOUGHT AND APPLICATION

1. What does the word – "standard" mean and imply – especially in spiritual matters? Is a standard supposed to be flexible and subject to individual interpretation? Why?

2. How does your definition compare with the secular understanding of what a "standard" is or isn't?

3. What makes God – God? (See – Psalm 102:25-27 – and – Malachi 3:6)

4. What is characteristic about Jesus Christ? (See – Hebrews 13:8)

Are either of these truths about God and Jesus Christ subject to erosion or adaptation?

5. In II Timothy 2:19 (NIV) – What is unequivocally stated about God?

6. What is the twofold inscription as it pertains to "God's solid foundation"?

7. Psalm 11:3 asks a vital question, namely, "…if the foundations are destroyed, what can the righteous do?" In our present culture, what are some of the foundations (Christian and Biblical Values) that are being eroded, diminished and headed toward being destroyed?

8. In a practical consideration of God's Standards, if something is Condemned by God, are we permitted to Condone it? In other words, if/when God establishes "Thou shalt not…" are

we permitted to be permissive and allow anything less than that Standard to be alright and acceptable?

What if it involves one's family member, does God permit any variance with His Standard in that situation? Why?

In our religious practice, are we allowing things that are unallowable by God? Are we condoning any aspect of what God clearly condemns?

Should we be either shocked or surprised that we are not being blest by God (will He bless the tolerance of that which He condemns)?

9. In terms of "eroding standards" and "Church Leadership", as a starting point - do we choose men who are similar to Stephen in Acts 6:3-4 – "Therefore, brethren, seek out from among you seven men of good reputation, full of the Holy Spirit and wisdom, whom we may appoint over this business; but we will give ourselves continually to prayer and to the ministry of the word." – or – do we select a nearest warm body or someone who is related to someone else in the church, etc.?

10. If - #9 - is how it is done, are we contributors to "the eroding standard" – or – are we endeavoring to do God's work in God's Way so that it will have God's blessing upon it and us?

if My people who are called by My name
will humble themselves, and pray and seek My face,
and turn from their wicked ways,
then I will hear from heaven,
and will forgive their sin and heal their land.
                                        II Chronicles 7:14 (NKJV)

Worship Indifference

A question that can validly be asked is: What in the world is the "Church" doing today? Another way of looking at this question might be: Does the world really care what the "Church" is doing today? In a day and time when arguments are raised politically about "under God" when it is omitted by a political leader when he recites The Pledge of Allegiance, or the continuing number of Abortions (now numbering more than 50 million since the Roe v. Wade decision in 1973) and the declining number of protests, or a diminishing emphasis upon the National Day of Prayer on the first Thursday in May each year — where is the voice of the Church? Where is the clarity of message and reason? Who is seriously raising the standard today — unashamedly and without fear?

Any number of churches can be entered today and the visitor will be totally lost in terms of what is going on and question or wonder what relevance all of that service had for him/her. Was it meaningful and purposeful? Did it impact one in terms of worship of the Living God and did one have the sense of being in the presence of God during his/her sojourn in that service? In other words, was it at all relevant? If not, why not? In a current issue of Leadership Weekly, May 2nd, 2011, a feature article is entitled: "The Problem with Pizzazz - Has Entertainment Replaced Scripture As The Center of Our Worship?" The interview is with Dr. Charles R. Swindoll who is the pastor of Stonebriar Community Church in Frisco, Texas. His observations and assessment should be given careful — maybe prayerful — consideration. He has authored many books on the Christian Life and Spiritual Growth. His latest book: "The

Church Awakening: An Urgent Call for Renewal, outlines the dangers when churches seek the world's affirmation and copy the world's methods. A senior editor with Leadership Journal spoke with Dr. Swindoll about the use of entertainment values in worship. Some of that interview includes the following - - -

"Early in your book you say that when the church becomes an entertainment center, biblical literacy is the first casualty. So why do you think the church has become so enamored with entertainment? "We live in a time with a lot of technology and media. We can create things virtually that look real. We have high-tech gadgets that were not available to previous generations. And we learned that we could attract a lot of people to church if we used those things. I began to see that happening about 20 years ago. It troubled me then, and it's enormously troubling to me now because the result is an entertainment mentality that leads to biblical ignorance. And alongside that is a corporate mentality. We're tempted to think of the church as a business with a cross stuck on top (if it has a cross at all). The prevailing attitude tends to be: "We really shouldn't look like a church... but...why do you want your church's worship center to look like a talk show set?"

"Martyn Lloyd-Jones said, "When the church is absolutely different from the world, she invariably attracts it. It is then that the world is made to listen to her message, though it may hate it at first." When a church is spending more on media than shepherding, something is wrong. I know one church that has 17 people on their media staff and only 12 on the pastoral staff. Some time ago a group of church leaders decided that they didn't want to be hated. They focused just on attracting more and more people. But if we're here to offer something the world can't provide, why would I want to copy the world?

There is plenty of television. There are plenty of talk shows. There are plenty of comedians. But there is not plenty of worship of the true and living God....

"You think it's rooted in a deep insecurity that we have as church leaders? Yes, I do. I think you've put your finger on it. We want a crowd to make us feel important and liked. But why is getting a crowd our focus? Jesus never suggested that crowds were the goal. He never addresses getting your church to grow. Never. So why is that the emphasis today? ...But everything must square with Scripture. We must make sure that new things actually help people grow in the truth, that they edify the saints and build them up. Will it equip them to handle the world around them? Will it form them into the kingdom of God rather than the kingdom of this world? In many cases we use new things because they are novel, not because they are helpful... I have been to church services...where the only people who knew the songs were the band. I'm not edified. I'm just watching a show. And they're not interested in teaching me the songs either. They just sing louder to make up for the fact that no one else is singing. Loud doesn't help. Why do they do that? Do you want me to be impressed with how loud you are singing, how accomplished you are? I'm not. I'm not here to be impressed with you. I'm here to fall back in love with Christ.

"Speak to the 35-year-old pastor leading a young, growing church. The ministry is focused on communicating the gospel and honoring Christ, but he wants to incorporate more technology and media. How does that pastor know how far to go? What are the red flags he and his team should look for? First, he needs to surround himself with people that ask the hard questions, people that are not all his own age. Second, he needs to study the Scriptures deeply and ask whether he can square what they're doing with what the Bible says should be their focus. Third, he should ask whether or not this the best use of our money and time. Would I spend my time better pouring over God's Word, in prayer, getting my heart right, mentoring younger men and women, and building into my staff? What investment of my time is going to lead others to say, "You know what, these people are so different; this is so refreshing; this is beautiful."? "...Ultimately what attracts the world to the church are sanctified people, filled with God, living in communion with him and one another, and not an entertaining show...It's called "the body."

As an older servant of the Lord and one who has been the Pastor of several churches covering more than 47 years, I have tried to share with younger men from time to time a passage from God's Word that has been very significant in the life of my wife and me. It is in one of our favorite Psalms – Psalm 37:23-26, "The steps of a man are established by the Lord, when he delights in his way; though he fall, he shall not be cast headlong, for the Lord upholds his hand. I have been young, and now am old, yet I have not seen the righteous forsaken or his children begging for bread. He is ever lending generously, and his children become a blessing." How can the younger minister get past the idea and concept of large and bigness in most facets of his relationship to a local church? The Call to be a Minister of God is clear and precise. In II Timothy 2:15-16 (ESV), the instruction is: "Do your best to present yourself to God as one approved, a worker who has no need to be ashamed, rightly handling the word of truth. But avoid irreverent babble, for it will lead people into more and more ungodliness..." In II Timothy 3:14-17 the instruction is: "But as for you, continue in what you have learned and have firmly believed, knowing from whom you learned it and how from childhood you have been acquainted with the sacred writings, which are able to make you wise for salvation through faith in Christ Jesus. All Scripture is breathed out by God and profitable for teaching, for reproof, for correction, and for training in righteousness, that the man of God may be competent, equipped for every good work." One additional word of instruction is given in I Timothy 1:18-19, "This charge I entrust to you, Timothy, my child, in accordance with the prophecies previously made about you, that by them you may wage the good warfare, holding faith and a good conscience..."

The Lord's call is never intended for God's servants to be focused on things and stuff. He is to be less concerned and anxious regarding the "pay package" then he is with whether or not those issuing the call are desirous of sharing in the task of ministry and willing to be trained to do it more effectively. It would be beneficial if the young minister could gently inquire from the calling church what they have determined to be the purpose of their church in the neighborhood where they are located and the demographic trend in the area of their location. In too many instances it is becoming more and more difficult to conduct a maintenance ministry, much less a church growth or renewal one.

It requires an honest approach and assessment. Can we be relevant where and how we are in the community of our location? Is there a ministry that can be done that will minister in a spiritual and Biblical way with those living around our church location? Do we want to reach our neighborhoods? Do we care about those who don't necessarily care about us or anything else? Can we determine ways that the love and compassion of Jesus Christ can be communicated by us and through us? Would we be willing to bring an non-churched near neighbor person into our home for a time of Fellowship (very often this can lead to an evangelistic opportunity)? Can we think of creative ways where we could be relevant that might spark some interest on the part of those we have purposed to reach?

These questions being posed require that those who govern a local church will be flexible and visionary. Some church boards are so entrenched in biased thinking and set in their historic way, that they refuse to expand their sphere of ministry in any way, shape or form. The younger Pastor needs to discern this from the beginning of the process of being interviewed and discussing who he is versus who or what the church is. He needs to be aware of how "set in their ways" people in the church can be. This is especially true where the governing board is comprised of the older members of the church. They have never paused to consider or reflected upon whether or not they have become intransigent. When that is the case, it is obvious they are in a rut. Someone has defined the proverbial rut that is so common throughout churches as being "...a grave with both ends kicked out..." This is one of the major reasons churches begin to lose ministry influence and gradually die.

A young man can visit church members and the sick; he can prepare excellent studies and preach his heart out; he can dot every "i" and cross every "t" exactly the way the governing board desires; he can put in long hours doing "church" work – but to what end? There will still be the gnawing issue of whether or not the church is growing. It will be the consensus of the governing board that the Pastor must not be working hard enough – if he did more there would be evidence of it and "our church" would be growing. The basic point here is in terms of understanding the Church – is it an "our church" mentality or is in a "God-Church" commitment?

One would do well to do a thorough, prayerful and objective study of Revelation – Chapters 1 through 3. Just a very brief summary here will set the tone and possibly whet some appetites to pursue the study. Revelation 1:10-20, The Apostle John writes: "I was in the Spirit on the Lord's day, and I heard behind me a loud voice like a trumpet saying, Write what you see in a book and send it to the seven churches, to Ephesus and to Smyrna and to Pergamum and to Thyatira and to Sardis and to Philadelphia and to Laodicea. Then I turned...I saw seven golden lampstands, and in the midst of the lampstands one like a son of man...In his right hand he held seven stars...When I saw him, I fell at his feet as though dead. But he laid his right hand on me, saying, Fear not, I am the first and the last, and the living one. I died, and behold I am alive forevermore, and I have the keys of Death and Hades. Write therefore the things that you have seen...As for the mystery of the seven stars that you saw in my right hand, and the seven golden lampstands, the seven stars are the angels of the seven churches, and the seven lampstands are the seven churches."

The One walking in the midst of the lampstands is the Bridegroom – the One Who purchased His Church through His shed blood and death on the cross – and Who declares: "I am the first and the last, and the living one. I died, and behold I am alive forevermore..." He comes and has definite requisites for His Church that cannot be modified or compromised. The Message from The Bridegroom to His Bride – His Church – is precise and unequivocal. While He observes each church in particular, there is an underlying general requirement, namely, "He who has an ear, let him hear what the Spirit says to the churches."

One could wonder how the particulars being pointed out could have been missed by the church. They had "their programs" in place; "their standards" clearly enunciated; "their routines" precisely established – isn't that enough? If the local church is trying to do what's right and good – why should there be any complaint? After all, "we've always done it this way" and there has been no objection to it. The analysis of the Church In Ephesus in Revelation 2:1-7 could easily be the application for most of the churches today. In Revelation 2:4-4, The Head of the Church – The Bridegroom – observes and states: "…But I have this against you, that you have abandoned the love you had at first. Remember therefore from where you have fallen; repent, and do the works you did at first. If not, I will come to you and remove your lampstand from its place, unless you repent…" There is a threefold requirement set before this Church that seemed to be doing everything decently and in order: (1) Remember; (2) Repent; (3) Return. Failure to comply and change will bring consequence of great significance and import, namely, "If not, I will come to you and remove your lampstand from its place, unless you repent…" The consequence is severe – removal of the lampstand from its place – no longer useful or functional in terms of The Bridegroom's agenda for His Church.

It's difficult to conceive that a "church" or individual could love The Bridegroom – Jesus Christ – less than at the initial moment when one passed from death into life. One's love is to increase as more of one's life is consecrated to the Lord. The "Church" is to be so in love with the Head of the Church that it would want to do everything possible to please and honor The Lord and Master. What has allowed for the coldness and indifference to replace the embers of warmth and assurance of being in fellowship with Jesus Christ? Has the church fallen in love with the culture that surrounds it and has grasped for the acceptance of the culture rather than seeking after the approval of Jesus Christ? What is the common denominator between the culture and Christ? What is the rationale of both the individual and the church for trying to co-mingle the two? There are two Biblical references that we must ponder in this regard. The first is Mark 8:34-37 where Jesus stated and asked, "If anyone would come after me, let him deny himself and take up his cross and follow me...For what does it profit a man to gain the whole world and forfeit (lose) his own soul? For what can a man give in return for his soul?" The Cross or the Culture – which one should be chosen? Physical gain versus the spiritual loss – which one should be selected? The second passage raises more questions that demand scrutiny and response. It is II Corinthians 6:14 – 7:1 (NLT) where Paul poses questions for the Corinthian church and professed believers to answer, "Don't team up with those who are unbelievers. How can goodness be a partner with wickedness? How can light live with darkness? What harmony can there be between Christ and the Devil ? How can a believer be a partner with an unbeliever? And what union can there be between God's temple and idols? For we are the temple of the living God. As God said: I will live in them and walk among them. I will be their God, and they will be my people. Therefore, come out from them and separate yourselves from them, says the Lord. Don't touch their filthy things, and I will welcome you...says the Lord Almighty."

This is serious stuff! The Lord wants a response from us – from His church. We can glean an insight of how Jesus Christ views those who would "straddle the fence" or who rationalize their faith so they can be more comfortable with their "Christian" persona. Revelation 3:14-17 contains these words to the church in Laodicea: "The words of the Amen, the faithful and true witness, the beginning of God's creation. I know your works: you are neither cold nor hot. Would that you were either cold or hot! So, because you are lukewarm, and neither hot nor cold, I will spit you out of my mouth…" Those who would choose to be lukewarm rather than being hot or cold are obnoxious and repugnant to the Lord. They become a negative taste or flavor to Him. He expectorates that which is lukewarm or indifferent to Him. The Lord will not tolerate anything less than total commitment and complete love. Would you want to be in His mouth when He decides who will be spewed out? Hopefully, you will have settled your choice so you will know and be assured that you are safe in the arms of Jesus.

Many church officers try to manage the work of the local church so it will be appealing to a greater number of people. The hope is that a moderate stance will be the bait on the hook that will cause others to be attracted to "their church." If only the "church" would change its ways and say to all: "We have not been right in our attitude and behavior. We have put our goals and preferences before the Lord's. We have compromised and tried to be accommodating so we might have a broader-based appeal. We have tried to do things our way rather than His way. We need to remember our first love moment with Jesus Christ and repent of what we have become and where we are today. We need to return to the Lord and that first love relationship and fellowship. Maybe the Lord will renew our lampstand purpose and give us a second chance – being what and who He wants us to be – and doing the work of His king-dom the way and manner in which He wants it done. As we make this course-correction, come join with us in our renewed commitment to Jesus Christ and His control of our life-journey with Him.

QUESTIONS FOR THOUGHT AND APPLICATION

1. What is your definition of the word "worship"?

2. At the "church" you regularly attend, what is your expectation for a "worship service"? Do you expect it to be contemporary or traditional; casual or formal; staid/stale or alive/refreshing; Hymn singing to accompaniment of a praise band or Organ/Piano; etc.?

3. In the "worship service", is the format more Form that is followed weekly or is it more Fluid? Is the service steeped in ritual and tradition? Is it predictable? Does it border on being "boring"?

4. In Chapter Five, there are a series of Assessment Questions raised. Let us consider and respond to them here...

Assessment Question 1:
Can we (the local "church") be relevant where and how we are in the community where we are located? How?

Assessment Question 2:
Is there a ministry that can be done that will minister in a spiritual and Biblical way with those living around our church location? If so, what would it be?

Assessment Question 3:
Do we want to reach our neighborhoods and near-neighbors? How have we tried?

Assessment Question 4:

Do we care about those who don't necessarily care about us or anything else? Where can these people be best reached?

Assessment Question 5:
Can we determine ways that the love and compassion of Jesus Christ can be communicated by us and through us? Give a few suggestions regarding how this can be done!

Assessment Question 6:
Would we be willing to bring a non-churched near neighbor into our home for a time of Fellowship (very often, this can lead to an evangelistic opportunity)?

Do we sometimes hesitate to invite the non-churched near neighbor or stranger into our home because of a fear that they may break, or soil, or steal our "stuff"?

Assessment Question 7:
Can we think of creative ways where we could be more relevant and that might spark some interest on the part of those we have purposed to reach?

God has not cast away His people whom He foreknew.
Or do you not know what the Scripture says of Elijah,
how he pleads with God against Israel, saying,
"Lord, they have killed Your prophets and torn down Your altars, and I alone am left, and they seek my life"?
But what does the divine response say to him?
"I have reserved for Myself seven thousand men
who have not bowed the knee to Baal."
                                    Romans 11:2-4 (NKJV)

Incline or Decline

The difference between an Incline and a Decline is simply direction. If it is heading upward, it is an Incline; if the direction is downward, it is a decline. The determining factor depends on the direction one wishes to go. If one happens to be in Chattanooga, Tennessee, one of the beautiful attractions is the Incline situated at the base of Lookout Mountain. When my children were young, one of their exciting moments was to ride the Incline on the Lookout Mountain Railway. The Incline is a funicular, in which two cars are attached to opposite ends of a fixed-length cable. The cars counter-balance each other so that the engine in the upper station needs to supply only enough power to overcome friction and the different weight of passengers in the two cars. Specially designed cars, with windows on the side and the ceiling, take passengers on the steepest passenger train ride in the world. Passengers are transported from St. Elmo's Station at the base, to Point Park at the mountain summit, which overlooks the city and the Tennessee River. The railway is approximately one mile in length (single track except for a short two-track stretch at the midway point, allowing operation of two cars at one time), and has a maximum grade of 72.7%. It is billed as the world's steepest passenger railway. While my children were excited with their fifteen minute ride to the top, their Grandmother was terrified for them. Needless to say, The Incline was built in 1895 and countless hundreds of tourists have taken that trip.

If a person is given to negative orientation, then most things in his/her world and life view can be characterized as Decline. On the other hand, a person with a positive perspective will be more apt to want to ascend further on the Incline. He doesn't dread the effort and exertion that will be required because he has a focus that is fixed on where he is headed and what he is seeking. This principle can be applied to nations and their approach to government, as well as to the "church" and it's diminishing focus on values that differentiate between the secular and the spiritual. Who is able to say today – "This is what 'The Church' believes and stands for as the rule and guideline for faith and practice?"

An illustration of the blurring views of "The Church" in the 21st Century is a found in the writings of Rob Bell in his book titled: Love Wins: A Book About Heaven, Hell, and the Fate of Every Person Who Ever Lived. In a promotional video regarding his book, Bell frames his thesis in this way: "Will only a few select people make it to heaven?...And will billions and billions of people burn forever in hell?...Millions and millions of people were taught that the primary message, the center of the gospel of Jesus, is that God is going to send you to hell unless you believe in Jesus. So what gets subtly sort of caught and taught is that Jesus rescues you from God. How could that God ever be good? ... And how could that ever be good news?...The good news is that love wins."

There is no shortage of critics when it comes to Rob Bell's thesis regarding heaven and hell. Some of the criticism states: Bell appears to be promoting universalism. Another states that Bell is preaching a false gospel. One terse criticism from an evangelical and reformed Pastor was simply: Farewell Rob Bell. In February 2011, Christianity included some of the above critiques and summarized: "Mars Hill pastor Rob Bell drew significant attention on Twitter and blogs today after Justin Taylor penned a blog post titled "Rob Bell: Universalist?" Taylor, vice president of editorials at Crossway, has not seen

Bell's book (though he read some chapters that were sent to him), but he expressed concern with a video. "This video from Bell himself shows that he is moving farther and farther away from anything resembling biblical Christianity," Taylor wrote. Taylor pointed to the publishers' description of the book, which does not come out until March 29 from Harper-One. "With searing insight, Bell puts hell on trial, and his message is decidedly optimistic—eternal life doesn't start when we die; it starts right now. And ultimately, Love Wins," part of the description states.

There is another book that contributes to the blurring of the focus regarding what "The Church" professes, practices promotes and proclaims. David Mays is one of the most prolific and reliable reviewers of publications that impact both World Missions and "The Church" as understood today. In June 2011, he reviewed a book titled: America's Four Gods - What We Say About God - And What That Says About Us by Paul Froese & Christopher Bader. David Mays summary of the book is: "Froese and Bader are professors of Sociology at Baylor University. They search for a sociological perspective on Americans' perceptions of God They interpret their research surveys and interviews to show that Americans see God as either engaged or disengaged with the world and either (primarily) judgmental or benevolent. This leads to "four Gods:" (1) The Authoritative God, who is both engaged with the world and judgmental; (2) The Benevolent God who loves and aids us in spite of our failings; (3) The Critical God, who catalogs our sins but does not punish them (at least not in this life); (4) The Distant God, who stands apart from the world. If God is the foundation of our worldview, then the kind of God we believe in is incredibly important. Our view of God affects how we view everything else, including society, morals, science, money, evil, and the future. The book provides insight on why Americans have such divergent perspectives..."

One can see how the writing of Froese and Bader can so easily attach itself to the writing of Rob Bell. Rob Bell would grasp the second view of God, namely, that He is "The Benevolent God who loves and aids us in spite of our failings." Regardless of what the "professionals" (Pastors, Professors, etc.) represent, the reality with the person in the pew is the same as what Rob Bell would grasp – God is "The Benevolent God who loves and aids us in spite of our failings." It would promote his conclusion that "love wins." It isn't the statement "love wins" that is really at issue but how it is used and applied by Rob Bell. He allows his definition of God to disallow the place prepared by God for the wicked who will be punished for eternity.

Just a brief glance in the New Testament regarding how Hell is discussed and applied. The Greek word – Gehenna – is the primary word behind what is being considered by Rob Bell. The World Dictionary defines Gehenna in the following manner: "In the Old testament, it is the Valley below Jerusalem where children were sacrificed in the fire and where idolatry was practiced (II Kings 23:10 and Jeremiah 19:6). It is also the place where later on offal (offal = the parts of a butchered animal that are considered inedible by human beings; refuse, rubbish, and garbage) were slowly burned. In the New Testament, it is a place where the wicked are punished or destroyed after the Resurrection of the Dead; a place or state of pain and torment."

In The Synoptic Gospels – Matthew, Mark, Luke – Jesus uses the word Gehenna eleven times to describe the opposite to life in the Kingdom. In Mark 9:43-48, "And if your hand causes you to sin, cut it off. It is better for you to enter life crippled than with two hands to go to hell, to the unquenchable fire. And if your foot causes you to sin, cut it off. It is better for you to enter life lame than with two feet to be thrown into hell. And if your eye causes you to sin, tear it out. It is better for you to enter the kingdom of God with one eye than with two eyes to be thrown into hell, where their worm does not die and the fire is not quenched." It is the place where both soul and body could be destroyed. In Matthew 10:28, "And do not fear those who kill the body but cannot kill the soul. Rather fear him who can destroy both soul and body in hell." It is in the "unquench- able fire" stated in Mark 9:43 where soul and body can be destroyed. Gehenna is also mentioned in James 3:6 where it is said to "set the tongue on fire" and the tongue in turn sets the entire course or wheel of life.

The complete list of references is as follows: Matthew 5:22 whoever calls someone "you fool" will be liable to Gehenna; Matthew5:29 better to lose one of your members than that your whole body go into Gehenna; Matthew 5:30 better to lose one of your members than that your whole body go into Gehenna; Matthew10:28 rather fear him who can destroy both soul and body in Gehenna; Matthew18:9 better to enter life with one eye than with two eyes to be thrown into Gehenna; Matthew 23:15 Pharisees make a convert twice as much a child of Gehenna as themselves; Matthew 23:33 to Pharisees: you brood of vipers, how are you to escape being sentenced to Gehenna?; Mark 9:43 better to enter life with one hand than with two hands to go to Gehenna; Mark 9:45 better to enter life lame than with two feet to be thrown into Gehenna; Mark 9:47 better to enter the kingdom of God with one eye than with two eyes to be thrown into Gehenna; Luke 12:5 Fear him who, after he has killed, has authority to cast into Gehenna; James 3:6 the tongue is set on fire by Gehenna.

Somewhere in all of these considerations – (1) Would or Could a Loving God send a soul to a literal Hell to be punished forever? – and – (2) Which God of the Four America's Gods would you prefer to make a determination regarding your eternal destination? – the Cross of Jesus Christ is being either forgotten or ignored. It was on that Cross that Jesus Christ was "wounded for OUR transgressions and bruised for OUR iniquities" (Isaiah 53:5). Forgotten in the overall discussion is: "For our sake he made him to be sin who knew no sin, so that in him we might become the righteousness of God." When He was made to be sin for us, meant that He bore the full penalty and judgment as our substitute (vicarious atonement) – the judgment and penalty that was rightfully ours He willingly and obediently took upon Himself – and allowed us to be the recipients of His righteousness (imputed to us).

Nave's Topical Bible does an exhaustive compilation of the use and meaning of Gehenna and includes a summary heading of: "The Future Home Of The Wicked" where he includes: "Psalms 9:17; Proverbs 5:5; Proverbs 9:13, Proverbs 9:15-18, 15:24; Proverbs 23:13-14; Isaiah 30:33, 33:14; Matthew 3:12; 5:29-30; 7:13-14; 8:11-12; 10:28; 13:30, 38-42, 50; 16:18; 18:8-9, 18:34-35; 22:13; 25:28-30, 41, 46; Mark 9:45-48; Luke 3:17; 16:23-26, 28; Acts 1:26; II Thessalonians 1:9; II Peter 2:4; Jude 1:6-23; Revelation 2:22; 9:1-2; 11:7; 14:10-11; 19:20; 20:10, 15; 21:8." In the discussion of Hell, one would be well advised to listen and be instructed by Jesus Christ, and to study and understand what the Holy Spirit inspired men of God to put into writing on the subject of Hell. While this Chapter is not intended as an exhaustive study on these theological matters of considerable importance, the words of the Holy Scriptures should give one pause before making new applications that will satisfy the present culture. A passage one should not avoid appears in Psalm 9:15-20 (NKJV), "The nations have sunk down in the pit which they made; In the net which they hid, their own foot is caught. The Lord is known by the judgment He executes; The wicked is snared in the work of his own hands. The wicked shall be turned into hell, And all the nations that forget God. For the needy shall not always be forgotten; The expectation of the poor shall not perish forever. Arise, O Lord, Do not let man prevail; Let the nations be judged in Your sight. Put them in fear, O Lord, That the nations may know themselves to be but men."

The world has had periods throughout history when the times were trying. One illustration of this is the year 1776 when Thomas Paine wrote some important words that have a bearing on all generations. The following paragraph was written by him in his pamphlet, "The American Crisis," He opened his famous pamphlet with these words: "These are the times that try men's souls. The summer soldier and the sunshine patriot will, in this crisis, shrink from the service of their country; but he that stands it now, deserves the love and thanks of man and woman. Tyranny, like hell, is not easily conquered; yet we have this consolation with us, that the harder the conflict, the more glorious the triumph. What we obtain too cheaply, we esteem too lightly: it is dearness only that gives every thing its value. Heaven knows how to put a proper price upon its goods; and it would be strange indeed if so celestial an article as freedom should not be highly rated." Paine knew that the nation of men would be one in a state of flux – one marked by continuous change, passage, instability or movement. Part of the concern of Paine was that the freedom purchased at such a great cost would be viewed too cheaply in and by future generations; that future generations would not share the same vision of freedom nor be willing to make the sacrifices to preserve and maintain it. He knew the consequences of compromise and wanted future generations to treasure freedom. Among those who became the Signers of the Declaration of Independence, the following is recorded about them: The signers of the Declaration of Independence pledged their lives, fortunes and sacred honor for the cause of freedom. Of those 56 who signed the Declaration of Independence, nine died of wounds or hardships during the war. Five were captured and imprisoned, in each case with brutal treatment. One lost his 13 children. Two wives were brutally treated. Twelve signers had their homes completely burned. Seventeen lost everything they owned. Yet not one defected or went back on his pledged word. Their honor, and the nation they sacrificed so much to create is still intact.

Throughout History, there are times when the Church has lost its direction and is actually in Decline (although those within the Church have been lulled into thinking they are on the Ascent rather than the Descent). Many have forgotten the foundational principles of The Reformation and the costs that men were willing to pay to establish a Church that knew freedom and liberty in Christ. One of the champions of The Reformation in the Church was Martin Luther. He made his thoughts known in a document that is historically known as The 95 Theses. His commitment to freedom and liberty in Christ can be sensed by the price he was willing to pay. When he was called upon to recant, he courageously stated: "Unless I am convinced by Scripture or by clear reasoning that I am in error – for popes and councils have often erred and contradicted themselves – I cannot recant, for I am subject to the Scriptures I have quoted; my conscience is captive to the Word of God. It is unsafe and dangerous to do anything against one's conscience. Here I stand, I cannot do otherwise. So help me God. Amen."

One of the places where he took his stand is seen in his persuasion that has been summarized: Martin Luther and the Reformers maintained that because of the depravity of man, no human authority could be trusted as absolute. He knew that - "Popes and councils have often erred and contradicted themselves." He rejected ecclesiastical totalitarianism and championed the principle of Sola Scriptura – The Bible alone is our ultimate authority. Anything apart from – Sola Scriptura – will bring about decline and/or delusional thinking. With his view of Scripture being so strong and needed as the foundation by which all matters of life and practice are to be measured, one wonders where the Martin Luther of today is who will call the Church back to its foundational principals.

Perhaps part of the problem stems from (a) what a person thinks of the Church and its teaching, or (b) a total lack of understanding of the importance of God's Word for all matters of faith and life. There are two places in the Bible where delusional thinking has allowed people to think "their Church" and "Church work" is in keeping with Biblical standards for spiritual health. In Matthew 7:21-23, Jesus tells those who boasted what they were doing in His name – "Not everyone who says to me, Lord, Lord, will enter the kingdom of heaven, but the one who does the will of my Father who is in heaven...I declare to them, I never knew you; depart from me, you workers of lawlessness." Paul gives a scathing assessment in II Thessalonians 2:9-12 – "The coming of the lawless one is by the activity of Satan with all power and false signs and wonders, and with all wicked deception for those who are perishing, because they refused to love the truth and so be saved. Therefore God sends them a strong delusion, so that they may believe what is false..." Being deceived they were on the Incline, they were blinded to the steep decline that was spiraling them downward. Jeremiah 23:12 spoke of it as a "slippery slope in the darkness" that can only result in disaster. The Message States it: "But they won't get by with it. They'll find themselves on a slippery slope, careening into the darkness, somersaulting into the pitch-black dark." The Prophets, Priests, and Shepherds were misleading the flock and the sheep were at the precipice of the "slippery slope" that would quickly result in their demise. The picture is given of the necessity for and the action of The Righteous Branch who will come because of the perverse condition stated in Jeremiah 23:1-4, "Woe to the shepherds who destroy and scatter the sheep of my pasture! declares the Lord. Therefore thus says the Lord, the God of Israel, concerning the shepherds who care for my people: You have scattered my flock and have driven them away, and you have not attended to them. Behold, I will attend to you for your evil deeds, declares the Lord. Then I will gather the remnant of my flock out of all the countries where I have driven them, and I will bring them back to their fold, and they shall be fruitful and multiply. I will set shepherds over them who will care for them, and they shall fear no more, nor be dismayed, neither shall any be missing, declares the Lord."

Jeremiah continues to declare the Lord's concern for His people and what the false prophets and priests have been doing to them. In Jeremiah 23:9-12, we read the Lord's awareness of and condemnation for them: "Concerning the prophets - My heart is broken within me; all my bones shake; I am like a drunken man, like a man overcome by wine, because of the Lord and because of his holy words. For the land is full of adulterers; because of the curse the land mourns, and the pastures of the wilderness are dried up. Their course is evil, and their might is not right. Both prophet and priest are ungodly; even in my house I have found their evil, declares the Lord.

Therefore their way shall be to them like slippery paths in the darkness, into which they shall be driven and fall, for I will bring disaster upon them in the year of their punishment, declares the Lord." The priests and prophets will experience ruin and death because of their neglect of duty and perversion of message for the sheep who needed care and guidance. The sheep were left on their own and had become scattered and prey for any predator.

The "church" today is dangerously close to the edge of the slippery slope. It's message is tainted. It has departed from the foundations and commitment required to function as "Christ's Church" versus "Man's Religious Club." The one's in positions of teaching and preaching ministry need the persuasion and commitment of the Apostle Paul. If only the "Church" and "Christian Community" of this day would wake up and review part of the cost of commitment for both life and proclamation. The words of the Apostle Paul are both stirring and challenging in Acts 20:24-27, "But I do not account my life of any value nor as precious to myself, if only I may finish my course and the ministry that I received from the Lord Jesus, to testify to the gospel of the grace of God. And now, behold...I testify to you this day that I am innocent of the blood of all of you, for I did not shrink from declaring to you the whole counsel of God." Can you identify with any of this commitment – "I do not account my life of any value; I do not count my life as precious to myself; I did not shrink from declaring to you the whole counsel of God - I have declared to you the whole counsel of God?"

What lessons has the "church" learned and what is it implementing for the sheep today? Some of the disturbing religious news in the year 2011 is this brief summary from The

Religious News Service in May 2011: More Than Fifty Churches Agree To Hold Qur'an Readings. The Berean Call has cited most of the following paragraphs, and they observe: "Even Atheists on occasion recognize that the real threat to them is not biblical Christianity, but Islam. Consider the comments below, prompted by an article from the Religion News Service printed in the Salt Lake Tribune: "...In the past I have stated I am not religious, but my goal is to help educate and unite Atheists and members of non-Islamic religions against a common enemy. That enemy is Islam. The good news is that our voice against Islam is clearly getting louder, the bad news is that far too many Americans who identify themselves as "Christians" are taking the easy way out and bowing down to Islam, in an effort to avoid a conflict that has been raging for 1400 years. Muslim Hadith Book 019, Number 4366: It has been narrated by 'Umar b. al-Khattib that he heard the Messenger of Allah (may peace be upon him) say: I will expel the Jews and Christians from the Arabian Peninsula and will not leave any but Muslim. A conflict in which Christians are clearly losing!" Pulpit pals writes: Christians, Jews, Muslims plan shared worship - "Religious and human rights activists are asking U.S. churches to invite Jewish and Muslim clergy to their sanctuaries to read from sacred texts next month in an initiative designed to counter anti-Muslim bigotry. The June 26 initiative, called Faith Shared: Uniting in Prayer and Understanding, is co-sponsored by the Interfaith Alliance and Human Rights First. Leaders of the two Washington-based groups said the event hopes to demonstrate respect for Islam in the wake of Quran burnings in recent months. More than 50 churches in 26 states already have committed to the initiative, including the Washington National Cathedral. Tad Stahnke, director of policy and programs for Human Rights First [said] 'that Americans do respect religious differences and reject religious bigotry and the demonization of Islam or any other religion'."

Obviously, we need to know the difference between being on the Incline versus tumbling down the Decline! Someone has rightly observe when writing: "Martin Luther wrote that Christians should be free of the arbitrary control of both church and state. God alone is the Lord of the conscience. Luther wrote: It is with the Word that we must fight, by the Word we must overthrow and destroy that which has been set up by violence. I will not make use of force against the superstitious and unbelieving... liberty is the very essence of Faith... I will preach, discuss and enlighten; but I will constrain none, for Faith is a voluntary act... I have stood up against the pope, indulgences and papists, but without violence or tumult. I put forward God's Word; I preached and I wrote – this was I all I did, the Word did all... God's Word should be allowed to work alone... it is not in my power to fashion the hearts of men... I can get no further than the ears; the hearts I cannot reach. And since I cannot pour faith into their hearts, I cannot, nor should I, force anyone to have faith. That is God's work alone, who causes faith to live in the heart... we should preach the Word, but results must be left solely to God's good pleasure."

Before exposing the "church" and "the flock" to the teachings and beliefs of other religions, the leaders of the church and flock need to be certain that they as leaders are well-grounded and that the flock is well-grounded in the whole counsel of God. Can your "church leader" say before the Head of the Church – Jesus Christ – that he has declared to the sheep the message of Jesus Christ – clear, precise and distinct. Is he able to say: "I did not shrink from declaring to you the whole counsel of God - I have declared to you the whole counsel of God?"

We must always remember what Jesus said in John 8:31-32, "So Jesus said to the Jews who had believed in him, "If you abide in my word, you are truly my disciples, and you will know the truth, and the truth will set you free."

Knowing and discerning between what is true and false is vital. Too many lack that discernment and ability to detect whether or not error is present in what they are being taught or what they may be reading. The words Paul brought to Timothy's thinking should be present with each of us. He wrote – II Timothy 2:15-17, "Do your best to present yourself to God as one approved, a worker who has no need to be ashamed, rightly handling the word of truth. But avoid irreverent babble, for it will lead people into more and more ungodliness, and their talk will spread like gangrene…" When the Secret service was first organized in 1865, their chief responsibility was the detection of counterfeit money. The way they were trained and prepared themselves for that important task was to study only the valid money printed by the United States Mint. When they knew what the authentic money from the mint was, they were easily able to detect that which was erroneous, false and counterfeit. Nowadays, there are other techniques such as watermarks and threads and codes, etc.

If guarding against the counterfeit in terms of currency required that dedicated preparation, should the handling of the Word of God and the teaching of God's sheep require anything less? The answer should be obvious! If anything, the words of II Timothy 2:15 should be emblazoned on the heart and mind of the prophets, priests and shepherds of our day – "Do your best to present yourself to God as one approved, a worker who has no need to be ashamed, rightly handling the word of truth." The Message translates II Timothy 2:14-17, "Repeat these basic essentials over and over to God's people. Warn them before God against pious nitpicking, which chips away at the faith. It just wears everyone out. Concentrate on doing your best for God, work you won't be ashamed of, laying out the truth plain and simple. Stay clear of pious talk that is only talk. Words are not mere words, you know. If they're not backed by a godly life, they accumulate as poison in the soul.>>" And in the New Living Translation, "Remind everyone of these things, and command them in God's name to stop fighting over words. Such arguments are useless, and they can ruin those who hear them. Work hard so God can approve you. Be a good worker, one who does not need to be ashamed and who correctly explains the word of truth. Avoid godless, foolish discussions that lead to more and more ungodliness. This kind of talk spreads like cancer..."

The one who has ears to hear – must hear! The one who has eyes to see – must see! The one who has a discerning mind – must discern! No one should be like a sponge that absorbs whatever comes ones way. Rather, knowledge of the Word of God must be so ingrained within one, that rather than absorbing any and all foreign teaching – one will be able to repel it by measuring it against the whole counsel of God. One needs to be like the Berean believers in Acts 17:11, "Now these Jews were more noble than those in Thessalonica; they received the word with all eagerness, examining the Scriptures daily to see if these things were so." In the New Living Translation, the verse is rendered: "And the people of Berea were more open-minded than those in Thessalonica, and they listened eagerly to Paul's message. They searched the Scriptures day after day to check up on Paul and Silas, to see if they were really teaching the truth." We would do well to do nothing less and to be completely persuaded by and grounded in the Word of God.

QUESTIONS FOR THOUGHT AND APPLICATION

1.   In both World and Biblical History, there have been distinct periods when the "Church" seemed to be in Decline. In the Old Testament, the children of Israel were subjected to at least three major captivities. List them and give a brief summary regarding why the captivity occurred? (Exodus, Isaiah, Daniel should give you some hints).

2.   If we understand "Incline" to mean Ascending and "Decline" to mean Descending, do you believe the "Church" today is "ascending" or "descending"? Why and in what ways?

3.   In Matthew 16:18, Jesus makes a dogmatic statement: "And I also say to you that you are Peter, and on this rock I will build My church, and the gates of Hades shall not prevail against it." In His day, was the "church" on the Incline or Decline? Explain your answer!

4.   Jesus was very clear about who was and wasn't a part of His Church.
In Matthew 7:21-23 - Jesus is explicit in terms of "who" will enter His Kingdom of Heaven. What is the singular basis on which one can be assured of entering God's Heaven?

In Matthew 25:31-46 - Jesus is separating the sheep from the goats. In this act of Jesus is the destiny for the sheep and goats. In Matthew 25:46, where do the sheep go? Where do the goats go?

What is the criteria by which this eternal determination is made (Sheep – Vss. 34-40; Goats – Vss. 41-45)?

A measure that is used with both the sheep and the goats refers to what was done or not done for "one of the least of these My brethren"! Who are some of the "least of these" in your community and neighborhood? Is there someone? Is there anyone?

Which group represented the Incline/Ascending and which group represented the Decline/Descending? In which group do you think Jesus would identify you?

5.   In Revelation 2 and 3, Jesus Christ is walking in the midst of the Seven Churches. He makes a Positive and Negative Statement regarding the particular Churches.

Example 1: Revelation 2:1-7 – The Church at Ephesus

- What does Jesus Commend the Church for having done?
- What does He point out as a blind spot in their ongoing work for Him and their relationship to Him?
- What is urgent for them to do immediately? Why?

Example 2: Revelation 3:7-12 – The Church at Philadelphia

- Does Jesus commend or condemn this Church?
- In terms of their resolve and purpose, what is it they had to do – and – did?
- What will he cause their antagonists – those of the Synagogue of Satan – come and do? What will they realize in that moment of time?

6.   With which one of these Seven Churches in Revelation 2 and 3 do you believe your church would most closely resemble

and identify? Why did you make that selection/choice? Do you identify your church as one being on (a) the Incline – Ascending or on (b) the Decline – Descending?

"Look among the nations and watch-- Be utterly astounded!

For I will work a work in your days

Which you would not believe, though it were told you.

Habakkuk 1:5 (NKJV)

Utter Darkness

The people dwelling in darkness have seen a great light, and for those dwelling in the region and shadow of death, on them a light has dawned. Matthew 4:16

There is nothing as dreadful and scary as the darkness. It seems to envelope one and causes many to have a sense of great fear. A question was asked: "What one place would you like not to be if there was a total power failure?" The greater number of people responded: "In an elevator!" Their answer conveyed the idea of one having the sense of being helpless and trapped. Children have vivid imaginations and develop a fear of the darkness – of something or someone lurking under a bed or in a closet. Parents attempt to compensate for that fear by reading wholesome stores to their children and then tucking them into bed. The psychology in doing this is to allow the child to have pleasant and positive thoughts rather than of goblins or ghosts ready to pounce. Night Lights have been common place through the generations. When I was a child, the night light was a small, round candle that was in a special candle cup. It served as the night light. Now there are the more sophisticated night lights that are plugged into a wall. They have a sensor that triggers the light to turn on as darkness descends.

One of the recollections I have from my youth centers in World War II. During the war, there were regular Blackouts held in major cities and all communities in the United States. Air Raid Wardens were assigned neighborhoods where the effort was put forth to make certain everyone complied with the Blackout requirement. The impression was how suddenly everything became darkened. The darkness was everywhere. Other precautions taken - Black Shades on windows were common place; the upper half of headlights were painted black to lesson the brightness of the light. The Darkness was a reality because safety was foremost. Light would provide the enemy with guidance to a target in a time of attack. In addition, air raid drills were held in the public schools so the children would be led to places of shelter in case of an attack. At that time, darkness was viewed as a necessity for safety and defense purposes.

Physical Darkness is understood and experienced by everyone. One of the phobias that is common to most is the Fear of Darkness. However, Physical Darkness is not the only darkness about which one is to have understanding. There is this brief statement in Matthew 4:16-17 that speaks of the reality of darkness from a completely different perspective – the spiritual darkness that prevailed. Note the words: "the people dwelling in darkness have seen a great light, and for those dwelling in the region and shadow of death, on them a light has dawned." These same words were prophesied in Isaiah 9:2, "The people who walked in darkness have seen a great light; those who dwelt in a land of deep darkness, on them has light shined." Matthew 4 continues: "From that time Jesus began to preach, saying, "Repent, for the kingdom of heaven is at hand." This is similar to a declaration in Isaiah 59:8-12, "...The way of peace they do not know, and there is no justice in their paths; they have made their roads crooked; no one who treads on them knows peace. Therefore justice is far from us, and righteousness does not overtake us; we hope for light, and behold, darkness, and for brightness, but we walk in gloom. We grope for the wall like the blind; we grope like those who have no eyes; we stumble at noon as in the twilight, among those in full vigor we are like dead men. We all growl like bears; we moan and moan like doves; we hope for justice, but there is none; for salvation, but it is far from us. For our transgressions are multiplied before you, and our sins testify against us..."

The words regarding darkness are descriptive: "The people dwelling in darkness..." – ensnared and entrapped – without hope – just fear and anxiety. "The way of peace they did not know..." – just turmoil and jeopardy. Isaiah shares this description: "We hope for light, and behold, darkness, and for brightness, but we walk in gloom. We grope for the wall like the blind; we grope like those who have no eyes; we stumble at noon as in the twilight, among those in full vigor we are like dead men. " Gloom...Groping...Stumbling...Like dead men.... What a description of hopelessness, fear and despair! They are left without a Moral Compass and have rejected the Word of God.

One example of the loss of a Moral Compass and the absence of the Word of God is part of the strategy of the spiritual warfare of the current day. There are many who are concerned over a report (CNSNews.com) on June 02, 2011 that is headlined: "Call to Ban the Bible Troubles Pakistan's Embattled Christians." The body of the report states: "Pakistani Christians reacted with dismay Thursday to campaign by radical Muslim clerics to have the Bible declared blasphemous and banned, but some said the community should respond calmly, without fear, trusting God to protect His word. Muslims should not blame Pakistan's Christian minority for the actions of one misguided pastor in Florida (Terry Jones), said one activist, who also noted that even Mohammed, the 7th century Muslim prophet, had not outlawed the Bible. A group of Muslim clerics has asked the Supreme Court of Pakistan to determine that certain passages of the Bible, violates the country's blasphemy laws because they depict some biblical figures – whom Muslims revere as "Islamic prophets" – as flawed or immoral. If the court does not make the declaration, the campaigners said, they would lodge a formal application for the Bible to be banned in its entirety...Aqeel said JUI-S should remember that, even during the times of Mohammed and the subsequent caliphs and other Muslim rulers, the Bible was not banned despite the fact that all of them knew that the Bible had different viewpoint on several things..." If such a demand becomes law, what does that mean in terms of Spiritual Darkness and Spiritual Light?

There were times when Scripture records that people had no place and no use for the Word of the Living God. While there was a pretense to look for The Word, it was not a sincere and diligent effort. One passage that addresses this plight and condition is Amos 8:9-12, "And on that day, declares the Lord GOD, I will make the sun go down at noon and darken the earth in broad daylight. I will turn your feasts into mourning and all your songs into lamentation; I will bring sackcloth on every waist and baldness on every head; I will make it like the mourning for an only son and the end of it like a bitter day. Behold, the days are coming, declares the Lord God, when I will send a famine on the land - not a famine of bread, nor a thirst for water, but of hearing the words of the LORD. They shall wander from sea to sea, and from north to east; they shall run to and fro, to seek the word of the LORD, but they shall not find it..." The time when God will allow the people to know the severity of their neglect of Him and His Word. Albert Barnes in his notes on the Bible states: "They shall wander – Literally - reel. The word is used of the reeling of drunkards, of the swaying to and fro of trees in the wind, of the quivering of the lips of one agitated, and then of the unsteady seeking of persons bewildered, looking for what they know not where to find. From sea to sea, from the sea of Galilee to the Mediterranean, that is, from east to west, and from the north even to the sun-rising, round again to the east, from where their search had begun, where light should be, and was not..." Barnes continues his thoughts by appealing to the prophet Ezekiel and a similar rejection and despising of God's Word. He writes: "The principle of God's dealings, that, in certain conditions of a sinful people, He will withdraw His word, is instanced in Israel, not limited to it. God says to Ezekiel, I will make your tongue cleave to the roof of your mouth, and you shall be dumb; and shall not be to them one who reproves, for it is a rebellious house - Ezekiel 3:26; and Ezekiel says, Destruction shall come upon destruction, and rumor shall be upon rumor, and they shall seek a vision from the prophet, and the law shall perish from the priest and counsel from the ancients - Ezekiel 7:26. God turns away from them, and checks the grace of prophecy. For since they neglected His law, He on His side, He stays the prophetic gift. And the word was precious in those days, there was no open vision, that is, God did not speak to them through the prophets; He breathed not upon them the Spirit through which they spoke. He did not appear to them, but is silent and hidden. There was silence, enmity between God and man."

Just think of the peril for the one who rejects the authority of God and His Law and Word. The description is of one staggering in darkness, reeling aimlessly, without any light for lamination or guidance. Some will even appeal to their memory of a time when the Prophet would speak with a vision from God but there will be nothing but silence. God and His word are silent and hidden. Matthew Henry's Concise Commentary personalizes when he writes regarding Amos 8:11-14,"Here was a token of God's highest displeasure. At any time, and most in a time of trouble, a famine of the word of God is the heaviest judgment. To many this is no affliction, yet some will feel it very much, and will travel far to hear a good sermon; they feel the loss of the mercies others foolishly sin away. But when God visits a backsliding church, their own plans and endeavors to find out a way of salvation, will stand them in no stead. And the most amiable and zealous would perish, for want of the water of life, which Christ only can bestow. Let us value our advantages, seek to profit by them, and fear sinning them away." The Message translates Amos 8:11-12, "Oh yes, Judgment Day is coming! These are the words of my Master God. I'll send a famine through the whole country. It won't be food or water that's lacking, but my Word. People will drift from one end of the country to the other, roam to the north, wander to the east. They'll go anywhere, listen to anyone, hoping to hear God's Word - but they won't hear it." What a horrendous judgment! What a foolish and costly error! How great a penalty for the neglect of God and rebellion against His Law and Word.

The condition of the people is very sinful before the Lord. The Prophet Isaiah records in Isaiah 59:1-15 (selected) how God sees and views His people and world: "Behold, the Lord's hand is not shortened, that it cannot save, or his ear dull, that it cannot hear; but your iniquities have made a separation between you and your God, and your sins have hidden his face from you so that he does not hear. For ...your lips have spoken lies; your tongue mutters wickedness. No one enters suit justly; no one goes to law honestly; they rely on empty pleas, they speak lies, they conceive mischief and give birth to iniquity...Their works are works of iniquity, and deeds of violence are in their hands. Their feet run to evil, and they are swift to shed innocent blood; their thoughts are thoughts of iniquity; desolation and destruction are in their highways. The way of peace they do not know, and there is no justice in their paths; they have made their roads crooked; no one who treads on them knows peace. Therefore justice is far from us, and righteousness does not overtake us; we hope for light, and behold, darkness, and for brightness, but we walk in gloom. We grope for the wall like the blind; we grope like those who have no eyes; we stumble at noon as in the twilight, among those in full vigor we are like dead men...we hope for justice, but there is none; for salvation, but it is far from us. For our transgressions are multiplied before you, and our sins testify against us; for our transgressions are with us, and we know our iniquities: transgressing, and denying the Lord, and turning back from following our God... conceiving and uttering from the heart lying words. Justice is turned back, and righteousness stands far away; for truth has stumbled in the public squares, and uprightness cannot enter. Truth is lacking, and he who departs from evil makes himself a prey."

Additionally, in Jeremiah 23:9-14 the Lord is looking at the plight and condition of His people and addresses how they got that way. One can only wonder about His view of what is called The Church – what have the prophets and priests and pastors been doing to God's flock? Note what He says through Jeremiah, "Concerning the prophets: My heart is broken within me; all my bones shake; I am like a drunken man, like a man overcome by wine, because of the LORD and because of his holy words. For the land is full of adulterers; because of the curse the land mourns, and the pastures of the wilderness are dried up. Their course is evil, and their might is not right. Both prophet and priest are ungodly; even in my house I have found their evil, declares the Lord. Therefore their way shall be to them like slippery paths in the darkness, into which they shall be driven and fall, for I will bring disaster upon them in the year of their punishment, declares the Lord. In the prophets of Samaria I saw an unsavory thing: they prophesied by Baal and led my people Israel astray. But in the prophets of Jerusalem I have seen a horrible thing: they commit adultery and walk in lies; they strengthen the hands of evildoers, so that no one turns from his evil; all of them have become like Sodom to me, and its inhabitants like Gomorrah." God can never – and will never – condone what He has condemned. Men can and do think otherwise – but – they err and do not know or speak the truth from God.

In Matthew 6, Jesus is giving a discourse and shares a model of Prayer for the disciples. He also gives instruction regarding the value and benefit of fasting along with one's praying. He then addresses what one treasures and where ones treasure ought to be. In Matthew 6:19-24, some of the words taught by Jesus Christ are: "Do not lay up for yourselves treasures on earth, where moth and rust destroy and where thieves break in and steal, but lay up for yourselves treasures in heaven, where neither moth nor rust destroys and where thieves do not break in and steal. For where your treasure is, there your heart will be also. The eye is the lamp of the body. So, if your eye is healthy, your whole body will be full of light, but if your eye is bad, your whole body will be full of darkness. If then the light in you is darkness, how great is the darkness…! Matthew 6:21-23 in The New Living Translation: "Wherever your treasure is, there your heart and thoughts will also be. Your eye is a lamp for your body. A pure eye lets sunshine into your soul. But an evil eye shuts out the light and plunges you into darkness. If the light you think you have is really darkness, how deep that darkness will be!" The emphasis is upon darkness – (a) how great is the darkness, and (b) how deep that darkness will be.

The twenty-first century appears to be a time when repudiation of God's Word seems to be escalating. The culture and the Church seem to have meshed and have left little room for God and His Word. As a matter of fact, many things being enacted into law are opposite to what God's Word has taught and the church is condoning the practices that God has forbidden in His Law. To argue that God's Law was for a different generation and time is too convenient for the present day that has excused itself from any obligation or obedience to the very One Who demands attention and His Word that demands compliance.

What awaits those who have repudiated the Authority of God in and for their lives, and the Word of God that has been given for ones instruction and obedience? II Peter 2:1-4, 9-10 gives us some idea: "But false prophets also arose among the people, just as there will be false teachers among you, who will secretly bring in destructive heresies, even denying the Master who bought them, bringing upon themselves swift destruction. And many will follow their sensuality, and because of them the way of truth will be blasphemed. And in their greed they will exploit you with false words...For if God did not spare angels when they sinned, but cast them into hell and committed them to chains of gloomy darkness to be kept until the judgment...the Lord knows how to...keep the unrighteous under punishment until the day of judgment, and especially those who indulge in the lust of defiling passion and despise authority. Bold and willful, they do not tremble as they blaspheme the glorious ones," Another reference is made to those who have disregarded the Lord in verse 17 – "For them the gloom of utter darkness has been reserved." Just think of the awfulness of "the gloom of utter darkness..." – the aloneness and the despair!

There is a similar and further description given in Jude 1:10-13 regarding those who made a deliberate choice to choose a way and direction other than what God had established for them - "But these people blaspheme all that they do not understand, and they are destroyed by all that they, like unreasoning animals, understand instinctively. Woe to them! For they walked in the way of Cain and abandoned themselves for the sake of gain to Balaam's error and perished in Korah's rebellion. These are hidden reefs at your love feasts, as they feast with you without fear, shepherds feeding themselves; waterless clouds, swept along by winds; fruitless trees in late autumn, twice dead, uprooted; wild waves of the sea, casting up the foam of their own shame; wandering stars, for whom the gloom of utter darkness has been reserved forever." Once again the reference is made to "the gloom of utter darkness...forever."

Revelation 20:7-10 look at the finality of the chief enemy of God's people throughout all generations. We read: "Satan...will come out to deceive the nations that are at the four corners of the earth...to gather them for battle; their number is like the sand of the sea. And they marched up over the broad plain of the earth and surrounded the camp of the saints and the beloved city, but fire came down from heaven and consumed them, and the devil who had deceived them was thrown into the lake of fire and sulfur where the beast and the false prophet were, and they will be tormented day and night forever and ever..." In verse 14-15, we read: "Then Death and Hades were thrown into the lake of fire. This is the second death, the lake of fire. And if anyone's name was not found written in the book of life, he was thrown into the lake of fire."

When Jesus began His earthly ministry, John 1:4-5 states, "In him was life, and the life was the light of men. The light shines in the darkness, and the darkness has not overcome it." The mission and ministry of Jesus was clearly established after He had been tempted by the devil in Matthew 4. In Matthew 4:16-17, "the people dwelling in darkness have seen a great light, and for those dwelling in the region and shadow of death, on them a light has dawned. From that time Jesus began to preach, saying, Repent, for the kingdom of heaven is at hand." The life lived in surrender to Jesus Christ and that is yielded to His authority knows the reality of II Corinthians 4:6, "For God, Who said: Let light shine out of darkness, made his light shine in our hearts to give us the light of the knowledge of God's glory displayed in the face of Christ." Ephesians 5:6-11 establishes a clear distinction between the darkness and light. Note what Paul has written: "Let no one deceive you with empty words, for because of these things the wrath of God comes upon the sons of disobedience. Therefore do not become partners with them; for at one time you were darkness, but now you are light in the Lord. Walk as children of light...and try to discern what is pleasing to the Lord. Take no part in the unfruitful works of darkness, but instead expose them." A further distinction is given in I Thessalonians 5:4-5, "But you...are not in darkness so that this day should surprise you like a thief. You are all children of the light and children of the day. We do not belong to the night or to the darkness."

It must always be remembered and practiced that the child of God "...does not belong to the night or to the darkness." The one who has come to Jesus Christ Who is The Light, must walk and live as a child of light because we no longer belong to the realm and sphere of the night or darkness. We embrace the Triune God in our worship and obedience, and we adhere to the Word of God as our only infallible rule for faith and practice. In regard to the Word of God and its place in and for ones life, Psalm 119:105 states: "Your word is a lamp to my feet and a light to my path." The Message translates verse 105, "By your words I can see where I'm going; they throw a beam of light on my dark path." In the spiritual application, removal of the Bible – God's Holy Word – darkness is the inevitability. In the secular application, any nation that bans the Bible – especially the Gospel – is a nation that has lost its moral compass. Nothing is adequate as a substitute for God's Word. II Timothy 3:16-17 states it clearly: "All Scripture is breathed out by God and profitable for teaching, for reproof, for correction, and for training in righteousness, that the man of God may be competent, equipped for every good work." We would do well to remember the refrain from an old Hymn:

The Bible stands though the hills may tumble,
It will firmly stand when the earth shall crumble;
I will plant my feet on its firm foundation,
For the Bible stands."

We would be wise to be among those who cherish and treasure God's Word! The foundation for ones faith is Jesus Christ – I Corinthians 3:11 – "For no one can lay a foundation other than that which is laid, which is Jesus Christ." We also have the foundation of God's Word. In Luke 6:47-48 we read: "Everyone who comes to me and hears my words and does them, I will show you what he is like: he is like a man building a house, who dug deep and laid the foundation on the rock… Two of my favorite Hymns contain words about the importance and place of the right foundation. One of them is, How Firm A Foundation…

How firm a foundation, ye saints of the Lord,
Is laid for your faith in His excellent Word!
What more can He say than to you He hath said,
You, who unto Jesus for refuge have fled?

Fear not, I am with thee, O be not dismayed,
For I am thy God and will still give thee aid;
I'll strengthen and help thee, and cause thee to stand
Upheld by My righteous, omnipotent hand.

When through the deep waters I call thee to go,
The rivers of woe shall not thee overflow;
For I will be with thee, thy troubles to bless,
And sanctify to thee thy deepest distress.

When through fiery trials thy pathways shall lie,
My grace, all sufficient, shall be thy supply;
The flame shall not hurt thee; I only design
Thy dross to consume, and thy gold to refine.

The soul that on Jesus has leaned for repose,
I will not, I will not desert to its foes;
That soul, though all hell should endeavor to shake,
I'll never, no never, no never forsake.

The other Hymn that has been sung to the glory of the Lord is The Church's One Foundation written by Samuel J. Stone in 1866...

The Church's one foundation Is Jesus Christ her Lord,
She is His new creation By water and the Word.
From Heav'n He came and sought her
To be His holy bride;

With His own blood He bought her
And for her life He died.

The Church shall never perish! Her dear Lord to defend,
To guide, sustain, and cherish, Is with her to the end:
Though there be those who hate her,
And false sons in her pale,
Against both foe or traitor
She ever shall prevail.

'Mid toil and tribulation, And tumult of her war,
She waits the consummation Of peace forevermore;
Till, with the vision glorious, Her longing eyes are blest,
And the great Church victorious
Shall be the Church at rest.

O happy ones and holy! Lord, give us grace that we
Like them, the meek and lowly,
On high may dwell with Thee:
There, past the border mountains,
Where in sweet vales the Bride
With Thee by living fountains Forever shall abide!

QUESTIONS FOR THOUGHT AND APPLICATION

1.   When you are alone in a physical place where there is an absence of light, what are the immediate thoughts and inner-feelings that you have?
Do you feel lost or confused?
Do you have a sense of fear or panic?
Why?

2.   In a spiritual sense, the Bible makes reference to darkness and utter darkness.
Psalm 107:9-15 – reference is made about those who "sat in darkness and in the shadow of death."
Why were they in darkness and the shadow of death?
In Vs. 13 – what did the people have to do?
In Vs, 14 – what did the Lord do in their behalf?
Jude 1
Vs 13 references "wandering stars for whom is reserved the blackness of darkness forever." Why is this their plight and eternal destiny?

3.   Even though there may be fear and dread regarding physical darkness, there is not the same fear and dread when it comes to spiritual darkness. In John 3:19-20, we read: "And this is the condemnation, that the light has come into the world, and men loved darkness rather than light..." What are the two reasons stated in John 3:19-20 indicating why mankind prefers darkness to the light?
(a) Vs. 19:
(b) Vs. 20:

4.   Why does the secular man/woman prefer darkness to light?

- Are they devoid of a Moral Compass for their lives?
- Have they allowed their conscience to become seared so that they no longer can discern between right and wrong, or good and bad?
- Are they consumed with narcissism/self-indulgence?

5.   Isaiah 59:8-12 describes the person who has chosen the pathway that leads into utter darkness.
What does such a person grope for?
In darkness, what is one thing they will never find/know?
What do people who have made this choice hope for versus what they find?

6.   What awaits those who love darkness when God's Judgment Day arrives? An old hymn – "I Dreamed That The Great Judgment Morning" – contains this stanza and refrain… Ask yourself whether or not this describes you or someone you should purpose to reach for Jesus Christ?

The moral man came to the judgment,
But self-righteous rags would not do;
The men who had crucified Jesus
Had passed off as moral men, too;
The soul that had put off salvation,
"Not tonight; I'll get saved by and by,
No time now to think of religion!"
At last they had found time to die.

Refrain:
And, oh, what a weeping and wailing,
As the lost were told of their fate;
They cried for the rocks and the mountains,
They prayed, but their prayer was too late.

Piercing the Darkness

In him (Christ) was life, and the life was the light of men. The light shines in the darkness, and the darkness has not overcome it...The true light, which enlightens everyone, was coming into the world. John 1:4-9

Can you imagine the early days of cave exploration and the spelunkers who risked life and limb to uncover the secrets of the dark cave? How many would have the courage to go where no one has been before and where the dangers could be insurmountable? Would you be willing to go on such a journey? What one thing would you insist upon before you would enter the mouth of the cave? In all likelihood, one of the pieces of equipment would be a Miner's Hat with a Light affixed to it. Prior to 1818, those who explored the caves and established mines depended on Lanterns or some crude device to provide illumination for the exploration. The greater the light – the lesser the risk!

For one's spiritual journey and quest, the need for light is even greater. Paul summarized it well in II Corinthians 4:3-4 when he wrote: "And even if our gospel is veiled, it is veiled only to those who are perishing. In their case the god of this world has blinded the minds of the unbelievers, to keep them from seeing the light of the gospel of the glory of Christ, who is the image of God." The Message Translation takes some liberties and renders these verses as: "If our Message is obscure to anyone, it's not because we're holding back in any way. No, it's because these other people are looking or going the wrong way and refuse to give it serious attention. All they have eyes for is the fashionable god of darkness. They think he can give them what they want, and that they won't have to bother believing a Truth they can't see. They're stone-blind to the dayspring brightness of the Message that shines with Christ, who gives us the best picture of God we'll ever get." Can you imagine anyone making the choice to follow the "fashionable god of darkness" rather than the "glorious Light of the Gospel in Jesus Christ? As incredible as it sounds and appears, multitudes head for the broad road and make the deliberate choice to ignore the narrow way that leads to the Light and eternal life. Jesus Christ spoke these words that are recorded in John 3:19-21, " And this is the judgment: the light has come into the world, and people loved the darkness rather than the light because their works were evil. For everyone who does wicked things hates the light and does not come to the light, lest his works should be exposed. But whoever does what is true comes to the light, so that it may be clearly seen that his works have been carried out in God."

The reason given for the wrong choice that people make is "people loved the darkness rather than the Light because their works were evil." By way of contrast, the right choice means – I John 1:5-7 – "This is the message we have heard from him and proclaim to you, that God is light, and in him is no darkness at all. If we say we have fellowship with him while we walk in darkness, we lie and do not practice the truth. But if we walk in the light, as he is in the light, we have fellowship with one another, and the blood of Jesus his Son cleanses us from all sin. The New Living Translation renders these verses very clearly: "This is the message he has given us to announce to you: God is light and there is no darkness in him at all. So we are lying if we say we have fellowship with God but go on living in spiritual darkness. We are not living in the truth. But if we are living in the light of God's presence, just as Christ is, then we have fellowship with each other, and the blood of Jesus, his Son, cleanses us from every sin."

The direction for the one who has committed his or her life to Jesus Christ becomes obvious and clear as the Word of God is studied. A passage such as Ephesians 5:6-15 (selected) establishes the priority and parameters for ones life. The text states: "Let no one deceive you with empty words, for because of these things the wrath of God comes upon the sons of disobedience. Therefore do not become partners with them; for at one time you were darkness, but now you are light in the Lord. Walk as children of light...and try to discern what is pleasing to the Lord. Take no part in the unfruitful works of darkness, but instead expose (reprove) them. For it is shameful even to speak of the things that they do in secret. But when anything is exposed by the light, it becomes visible, for anything that becomes visible is light...Look carefully then how you walk, not as unwise but as wise," This means that each child of God is responsible to maintain the personal discipline of walking in the light and avoiding all the allurements and deeds of darkness. Don't allow for any innate curiosity to cause you to swerve from the narrow path. Many years ago, I read a Bible Commentary on the Gospel of Matthew and there was an observation shared on Matthew 7:13-14 - "Enter by the narrow gate. For the gate is wide and the way is easy that leads to destruction, and those who enter by it are many. For the gate is narrow and the way is hard that leads to life, and those who find it are few." The observation was: "The restrictions of the narrow way are not meant as infringements upon ones liberty but as protections from evil." I continue to be grateful for a Sunday School teacher who had his class of boys memorize and review frequently Psalm 1 – "Blessed is the man who (a) does not walk in the counsel of the ungodly, and who (b) does not stand in the pathway of sinners, and who (c) does not sit in the seat of the scorners." His instruction was in terms of the progression if one allows for any compromise, namely – listening to ungodly counsel; finding friendships and comfort while standing with sinners; and finally, sitting down among those who reject the Gospel and mock the Savior. Such enticement and appeal should scream out to us – DANGER! STAY AWAY!

When I was a child, before God was expelled from the Public Schools, one of the musical selections we learned was based upon Psalm 27, The Lord Is My Light and My Salvation. Some of the words contained in Psalm 27:1-4 are: "The Lord is my light and my salvation; whom shall I fear? The Lord is the stronghold of my life; of whom shall I be afraid? When evildoers assail me to eat up my flesh, my adversaries and foes, it is they who stumble and fall. Though an army encamp against me, my heart shall not fear; though war arise against me, yet I will be confident. One thing have I asked of the LORD, that will I seek after: that I may dwell in the house of the LORD all the days of my life, to gaze upon the beauty of the LORD and to inquire in his temple…." The Music Teacher had us to emphasize the words – "THE LORD" – as we sang the anthem. The emphasis that I would give it today is – THE LORD is MY LIGHT and MY SALVATION!

The description of Heaven could easily be summarized as The Place of Continuous Light. This is true because Jesus Christ is the Light that lights that place. Revelation 21:23-29 gives us a visual - a picture of heaven: "And the city has no need of sun or moon to shine on it, for the glory of God gives it light, and its lamp is the Lamb. By its light will the nations walk, and the kings of the earth will bring their glory into it, and its gates will never be shut by day--and there will be no night there. They will bring into it the glory and the honor of the nations. But nothing unclean will ever enter it, nor anyone who does what is detestable or false, but only those who are written in the Lamb's book of life." A recent anthem written by Walt Harrah captures the essence of Heaven and it is expressed beautifully and dramatically - No More Night.

The timeless theme,
Earth and Heaven will pass away.
It's not a dream,
God will make all things new that day.
Gone is the curse from which I stumbled and fell.
Evil is banished to eternal hell.

No more night. No more pain.
No more tears. Never crying again.
And praises to the great "I AM."
We will live in the light of the risen Lamb.

See all around, now the nations bow down to sing.
The only sound is the praises to Christ, our King.
Slowly the names from the book are read.
I know the King, so there's no need to dread.

No more night. No more pain.
No more tears. Never crying again.
And praises to the great "I AM."
We will live in the light of the risen Lamb.

See over there, there's a mansion, oh,
that's prepared just for me,
Where I will live with my Savior eternally.

No more night. No more pain.
No more tears. Never crying again.

And praises to the great "I AM."
We will live in the light of the risen Lamb.

All praises to the great "I AM."
We're gonna live in the light of the risen Lamb.

This place called Heaven, what is it like and what can one expect when arriving there? As Jesus prepared His disciples for His death and ascension, and this place called Heaven, He said (John 14:1-3),
"Let not your hearts be troubled. Believe in God; believe also in me. In my Father's house are many rooms. If it were not so, would I have told you that I go to prepare a place for you? And if I go and prepare a place for you, I will come again and will take you to myself, that where I am you may be also."
The new Living Translation is:
"Don't be troubled. You trust God, now trust in me. There are many rooms in my Father's home, and I am going to prepare a place for you. If this were not so, I would tell you plainly. When everything is ready, I will come and get you, so that you will always be with me where I am."

Jesus is teaching His disciples about a place called Heaven. At the very least: (1) Heaven Is A Particular Place. Notice the references to "you/your" in the text. As He speaks about Heaven, Jesus has "you" on His mind. "Let not your hearts be troubled. You Believe in God; believe also in me. In my Father's house are many rooms. If it were not so...I Would Have Told You So!! This Place Called Heaven - Early in His Ministry, When Jesus Taught His Disciples How They Could/Should Pray – What was The Focus He Wanted Them To Have? It was: "Our Father, Who art in Heaven; Hallowed Be Thy Name.." Additionally, Jesus wanted His followers to know that (2) Heaven Is A Prepared Place. Jesus has obligated Himself to "go and prepare a place for you." It is unique and special because He is the Chief Architect for this place called Heaven. He – Personally – Has Purchased That Place For You. The question is: How Can You Receive It? Regardless of what one may think, it is received only on the basis of the love, mercy and grace of God.

Jesus also wanted his followers to know that (3) Heaven Is A Promised Place. "I will come again and will take you to myself, that where I am you may be also." It is very unique in that no one deserves to go there; no one can earn his way there; and no one can purchase a place there. Jesus employs an interesting phrase when He speaks of the place He is preparing for His own (NLT) – "when everything is ready" – At that time – when everything is ready - one leaves this planet and enters into eternity to be in the Presence of the Triune God forever! The major consideration and concern is whether or not one is ready to exit this planet and enter into eternity. In this regard, an older Hymn written by P.P. Bliss includes this stanza:

Almost persuaded now to believe;
Almost persuaded Christ to receive;
Seems now some soul to say, Go, Spirit, go Thy way,
Some more convenient day On Thee I'll call.

Words in this hymn "Almost Persuaded" contain some of the excuses and rationale of many who delay any concern for their soul and eternity. It is a shame and tragedy that one would delay to the "some more convenient day" the destiny of his soul rather than to choose now the certainty, hope and assurance that allows one to know that "to be absent from the body" will mean that one is "present with the Lord. How different are the words in the Hymn written in 1871 from the words of a contemporary anthem written by Don Wyrtzen, in

1971, words that are very compelling and definitive. The Anthem is entitled: Finally Home - - -

> When engulfed by the terror of the tempestuous sea,
> Unknown waves before you roll;
> At the end of doubt and peril is eternity,
> Though fear and conflict seize your soul.
>
> When surrounded by the blackness of the darkest night,
> O how lonely death can be;
> At the end of this long tunnel is a shining light,
> For death is swallowed up in victory!
> Refrain:
> But just think - -
> Of stepping on shore – And finding it Heaven!
> Of touching a hand – And finding it God's!
> Of breathing new air – And finding it celestial!
> Of waking up in glory – And finding it home!

There are meaningful examples of those who persevered amid trying circumstances. They were sustained by their hope. One of these examples is Job. In the midst of his considerable suffering and losses, he was able to look beyond his immediate circumstances. He exclaims from the depths of his soul – Job 19:23-27 – "Oh that my words were written! Oh that they were inscribed in a book! Oh that with an iron pen and lead they were engraved in the rock forever! For I know that my Redeemer lives, and at the last he will stand upon the earth. And after my skin has been thus destroyed, yet in my flesh I shall see God, whom I shall see for myself, and my eyes shall behold, and not another. My heart faints within me!"

His comfort as he thinks about what God's plan and purpose is for his life, that if he dies, he'll know fully and completely what it means to be one who is - - -

Stepping on shore – and finding it Heaven!
Of touching a hand – and finding it God's!
Of breathing new air – and finding it celestial!
Of waking up in glory – and finding it home!

In much the same manner, the Apostle Paul echoed similarly his sense of death and eternity. He describes the place called heaven in these excerpts taken from II Corinthians 5:1-10 (NLT), "…we know that when this earthly tent we live in is taken down -- when we die and leave these bodies -- we will have a home in heaven, an eternal body made for us by God himself and not by human hands. We grow weary in our present bodies, and we long for the day when we will put on our heavenly bodies like new clothing. For we will not be spirits without bodies, but we will put on new heavenly bodies. Our dying bodies make us groan and sigh, but it's not that we want to die and have no bodies at all. We want to slip into our new bodies so that these dying bodies will be swallowed up by everlasting life. God himself has prepared us for this, and as a guarantee he has given us his Holy Spirit. So we are always confident, even though we know that as long as we live in these bodies we are not at home with the Lord. That is why we live by believing and not by seeing. Yes, we are fully confident, and we would rather be away from these bodies, for then we will be at home with the Lord. So our aim is to please him always, whether we are here in this body or away from this body. For we must all stand before Christ to be judged. We will each receive whatever we deserve for the good or evil we have done in our bodies."

This is the blessed hope of the child of God – when life is ended, he/she will be safe in the arms of Jesus forever. For Paul, it meant nothing more nor anything less than – whether through death, or by the second coming of Jesus Christ – Being In The presence with the Lord forever. It bears out the words of hope and assurance in the Anthem - - -

Of stepping on shore – and finding it Heaven!
Of touching a hand – and finding it God's!
Of breathing new air – and finding it celestial!
Of waking up in glory – and finding it home!

The Apostle Paul longed for the heavenly home and wrestled within himself regarding this matter. He shared in Philippians 1:21-28 his inner thoughts and rationale in these words, "For to me to live is Christ, and to die is gain. If I am to live in the flesh, that means fruitful labor for me. Yet which I shall choose I cannot tell. I am hard pressed between the two. My desire is to depart and be with Christ, for that is far better. But to remain in the flesh is more necessary on your account. Convinced of this, I know that I will remain and continue with you all, for your progress and joy in the faith, so that in me you may have ample cause to glory in Christ Jesus, because of my coming to you again. Only let your manner of life be worthy of the gospel of Christ, so that whether I come and see you or am absent, I may hear of you that you are standing firm in one spirit, with one mind striving side by side for the faith of the gospel, and not frightened in anything by your opponents..." The key to what he is sharing is in these words: "I am hard pressed between the two. My desire is to depart and be with Christ, for that is far better. But to remain in the flesh is more necessary on your account."

To wrestle with death is understandable. Every child of God has the Blessed Hope – Absence from the body is to be present with the Lord. The wrestling occurs as one thinks of those who will be left behind and the sorrow they will have and the loneliness they will sense. To leave ones spouse, children, family, grand-children, countless friends behind has one with the dilemma of Paul - "I am hard pressed between the two. My desire is to depart and be with Christ, for that is far better. But to remain in the flesh is more necessary on your account" - is part of the reason for the inner wrestling and tension. It is a good thing that all of this is in God's hands because His timing is perfect and His concern for those left behind will be continuous. I guess many long for the rapture of the Bride of Christ so we can all enter the presence of the Lord Jesus Christ together and forever.

One of the things every child of God needs to remember about death and separation comes from the beautiful and meaningful words in Acts 13:36 - "For David, after he had served the purpose of God in his own generation, fell asleep and was buried…" The Westminster Confession of Faith and Catechisms share with us these truths regarding – What happens to a believer when he dies?

The Shorter Catechism 37 asks and answers:
Q. What benefits do believers receive from Christ at death?
A. The souls of believers are at their death made perfect in holiness, and do immediately pass into glory; and their bodies, being still united to Christ, do rest in their graves till the resurrection.

Scripture Passages that undergird this response are - II Corinthians 5:6-8 - "Therefore we are always confident, knowing that, while we are at home in the body, we are absent from the Lord: (for we walk by faith, not by sight:) we are confident, I say, and willing rather to be absent from the body, and to be present with the Lord." 1 Thessalonians 4:14 - "For if we believe that Jesus died and rose again, even so them also which sleep in Jesus will God bring with him."

Further explanation and amplification is given in The Westminster Larger Catechism, Questions 84 through 86; and The Westminster of Faith, Chapter 33, Paragraph 1.

Another Creedal statement - The Heidelberg Catechism - has this meaningful and helpful statement in Question and Answer Number 1:

Q. What is thy only comfort in life and death?

A. That I with body and soul, both in life and death, (a) am not my own, (b) but belong unto my faithful Savior Jesus Christ; (c) who, with his precious blood, has fully satisfied for all my sins, (d) and delivered me from all the power of the devil; (e) and so preserves me (f) that without the will of my heavenly Father, not a hair can fall from my head; (g) yea, that all things must be subservient to my salvation, (h) and therefore, by his Holy Spirit, He also assures me of eternal life, (i) and makes me sincerely willing and ready, henceforth, to live unto him. (j)

Two of the many Scripture Passages that support this response are: Romans 14:7 – "For none of us lives to himself, and no man dies to himself." Romans 14:8 – "For whether we live, we live unto the Lord; and whether we die, we die unto the Lord: whether we live therefore, or die, we are the Lord's."

In Revelation 21:1-7, John shares this vision of what will occur at the New Heaven and New Earth - - "Then I saw a new heaven and a new earth, for the first heaven and the first earth had passed away, and the sea was no more. And I saw the holy city, new Jerusalem, coming down out of heaven from God, prepared as a bride adorned for her husband. And I heard a loud voice from the throne saying, Behold, the dwelling place of God is with man. He will dwell with them, and they will be his people, and God himself will be with them as their God. He will wipe away every tear from their eyes, and death shall be no more, neither shall there be mourning, nor crying, nor pain anymore, for the former things have passed away. And he who was seated on the throne said, Behold, I am making all things new. Also he said, Write this down, for these words are trustworthy and true. And he said to me, It is done! I am the Alpha and the Omega, the beginning and the end. To the thirsty I will give from the spring of the water of life without payment. The one who conquers will have this heritage, and I will be his God and he will be my son."

These concluding words remind one of II Corinthians 6:17-18, "Therefore go out from their midst, and be separate from them, says the Lord, and touch no unclean thing; then I will welcome you, and I will be a Father to you, and you shall be sons and daughters to me, says the Lord Almighty." It is fully understandable in terms of the intent of II Corinthians 7:1, "Since we have these promises, beloved, let us cleanse ourselves from every defilement of body and spirit, bringing holiness to completion in the fear of God." In considering "these promises", are you standing on the promises of God or are you resting upon a set of man-made premises?

The old Hymn writer, R. Kelso Carter, expressed as simply as possible the focus and commitment one must have and maintain as he reflects upon God and the promise of His Heaven. May these words represent your focus and commitment - - -

Standing on the promises of Christ my King,
Through eternal ages let His praises ring,
Glory in the highest, I will shout and sing,
Standing on the promises of God.

Standing on the promises that cannot fail,
When the howling storms of doubt and fear assail,
By the living Word of God I shall prevail,
Standing on the promises of God.

Standing on the promises of Christ the Lord,
Bound to Him eternally by love's strong cord,
Overcoming daily with the Spirit's sword,
Standing on the promises of God.

Standing on the promises I cannot fall,
Listening every moment to the Spirit's call
Resting in my Savior as my all in all,
Standing on the promises of God.

When one begins to Stand On The Promises of God, that is a testimony to the reality that one is Taking A Serious God Seriously. Are you able to sing this Hymn as a testimony of what you believe and where you are positionally with Christ, the King? Are you a demonstration and witness of what it means to be Taking A Serious God Seriously? May God grant that for each of us who identify ourselves with the name of His Son when we call ourselves "Christ"-ians!

QUESTIONS FOR THOUGHT AND APPLICATION

1.   When darkness prevails, what is the one thing any rational person would desire?

2.   If a person desires to dispel physical darkness, what must he/she tap into or be attached to?

3.   In John 1:4-9, we are told that Jesus Christ would be the source of at least two things. What are they?

4.   In I John 1:5-7, instruction is given regarding the best way for one to dispel spiritual darkness. There are certain criteria one must receive. Indicate what they are - - -

(a)   Vs 5: What do we learn about God?

(b)   Vs. 6: What is the condition if one is to have fellowship with God?

(c)   Vs. 7: Where does one have to walk – and – what will Jesus Christ do for such a one?

5.   If one was isolated or lost in pitch blackness, a beam of light piercing the darkness would be welcomed and allow one to have hope of rescue and deliverance. The condition and plight of those in darkness is stated in Isaiah 59:9-10 - - -
"Therefore justice is far from us, Nor does righteousness overtake us; We look for light, but there is darkness! For brightness, but we walk in blackness! We grope for the wall like the blind, And we grope as if we had no eyes; We stumble at noonday as at twilight; We are as dead men in desolate places."

The remedy for those isolated and lost in darkness is given in Isaiah 9:2. What have the people seen and how does it dramatically change their situation and condition?

This text is repeated in Matthew 4:16-17 and identifies Who can bring about the change for people's lives. What must a person do and why must he/she do it?
Ephesians 5:6-17 (NKJV) references the contrast between a spiritual life of darkness and a spiritual life of being in the light. Please read this passage of Scripture and answer the following:

(a)   What is one who is light in the Lord supposed to do?
(b)   What is the child of God obligated to find?
(c)   What must a child of the light avoid having and doing?
(d)   Why is this avoidance stipulated and required?
(e)   Who is the Source of The Light?
(f)   How should one walk? What exactly does this mean?
(g)   What must the child of light understand?

6.   How can you ascertain the pathway of Light day by day? Read Psalm 119:105. What is the best way to proceed as a child of the light? God's Word serves as what for us who believe?

Happy are those who hear the joyful call to worship,
for they will walk in the light of your presence, LORD.
Psalm 89:15 (NLT)

The Brilliant Light

You are the God who works wonders; you have made known your might among the peoples. You with your arm redeemed your people...When the waters saw you, O God, when the waters saw you, they were afraid; indeed, the deep trembled. The clouds poured out water; the skies gave forth thunder; your arrows flashed on every side. The crash of your thunder was in the whirlwind; your lightnings lighted up the world; the earth trembled and shook. Your way was through the sea, your path through the great waters; yet your footprints were unseen.   Psalm 77:14-19

The experience most have had with brilliant light is during a thunderstorm at nighttime. A jagged beam of bright and brilliant light flashes in the dark sky – frightening some and startling others. It appears suddenly and lasts but a fraction of a moment. The Encyclopedia Britannica describes lightning for us. It is a: "Visible discharge of electricity when part of the atmosphere acquires enough electrical charge to overcome the resistance of the air. During a thunderstorm, lightning flashes can occur within clouds, between clouds, between clouds and air, or from clouds to the ground. Lightning is usually associated with cumulonimbus clouds (thunderclouds) but also occurs in nimbostratus clouds, in snowstorms and dust storms, and sometimes in the dust and gases emitted by a volcano. A typical lightning flash involves a potential difference between cloud and ground of several hundred million volts. Temperatures in the lightning channel are on the order of 30,000 K (50,000 °F). A cloud-to-ground flash comprises at least two strokes: a pale leader stroke that strikes the ground and a highly luminous return stroke. The leader stroke reaches the ground in about 20 milliseconds; the return stroke reaches the cloud in about 70 microseconds. The thunder associated with lightning is caused by rapid heating of air along the length of the lightning channel. The heated air expands at supersonic speeds. The shock wave decays within a meter or two into a sound wave, which, modified by the intervening air and topography, produces a series of rumbles and claps."

The Psalmist observed and marveled (Psalm 77:18) when contemplating a display of God's power – "…your lightnings lighted up the world; the earth trembled and shook…" There is occasional damage caused by a bolt of lightning. In the year 2000, Dr. Ronald B. Standler wrote an essay regarding Damage Caused By Lightning and summarized: "Lightning causes damage to buildings and equipment in three different ways. (1) There can be damage as a result of a direct lightning strike. Such damage includes damage to roofing materials, structures such as chimneys, heating or air conditioning units located on the roof or exterior of a building, or fires caused by lightning igniting combustible material, such as wood-frame buildings or flammable liquids or vapors. (2) Part of the lightning current can be carried inside a building by electric power, telephone, analog or digital data lines (e.g., closed circuit television cameras, sensors in an industrial plant, etc.). This direct injection of lightning current inside a building can cause immense damage to electrical – and especially electronic – circuits and equipment. (3) The electromagnetic fields from the current in a lightning stroke can induce currents and voltage in wire and cables inside a building. Such surge currents are typically less intense than direct injection of current, but can easily vaporize integrated circuits in computers, modems, electronic control circuits…Electronic equipment is typically designed to operate in a well-controlled electrical environment. It is the responsibility of the user to install lightning protection, electrical surge-protective devices, and power conditioning equipment to mitigate the effects of disturbances in the electrical voltage waveform. It is well recognized that the trend toward integrated circuits with more transistors per unit area, and faster switching speeds, makes these circuits more vulnerable to both upset and damage. (A) Upset is a temporary malfunction without any physical change in the devices or equipment. For example, one might recover from upset by rebooting a computer; the only loss would be data that was not written to disk before the upset occurred, and consequential damages from the interruption of continuous operations. The consequential damages can be large, for example, in medical equipment used in life-support applications. (B) Damage is a permanent alteration in the physical properties of one or more components, that requires repair or replacement before the equipment can resume normal operation. Examples of lightning damage to electrical equipment include flashover of insulation inside motors or transformers, so that the equipment is no longer functional. Examples of lightning damage to electronic equipment includes vaporized traces on printed circuit boards, vaporized transistors and integrated circuits, blown fuses..."

Most have an idea of the history behind the discovery of Electricity. One of the early explorations into this study was conducted by Benjamin Franklin. In addition to his being one of the Founding Fathers of the United States of America, he was also a scientist who became a major figure in the American Enlightenment and the History of Physics for his discoveries and theories regarding electricity. In addition to his pursuits and studies regarding Electricity, he also is credited with the invention of The Lightning Rod; Bifocals; the Franklin Stove; and A Carriage Odometer. He is also credited with forming the first public lending Library in America, and the formation of the first Fire department in Pennsylvania. His early studies about electricity led him to some basic conclusions. He suspected that lightning was an electrical current in nature, and he wanted to see if he was right. One way to test his idea would be to see if the lightning would pass through metal. He decided to use a metal key and looked around for a way to get the key up near the lightning. Most already know, he used a child's toy, a kite, to prove that lightning is really a stream of electrified air, known today as plasma. His famous stormy kite flight in June of 1752 led him to develop many of the terms that we still use today when we talk about electricity: battery, conductor, condenser, charge, discharge, uncharged, negative, minus, plus, electric shock, and electrician. Franklin understood that lightning was very powerful, and he also knew that it was dangerous. That's why he also figured out a way to protect people, buildings, and ships from it, the lightning rod."

Electricity is one of those common things one takes for granted. We flip a switch = push a button – pull a string and expect that lights will come on, fans will blow, stoves will cook, Televisions will show a picture, Radios will play, etc. How it works does not concern too many. The main focus is whether or not it works at all. If we experience a power failure, one can call the Electric Company and they have the capability of pinpointing where the outage is located and what has occurred to cause it. We take it for granted that it will be remedied quickly and electrical power will be restored. If the electricity is off for an extended period of time, some panic – and worry – over refrigeration, freezers, and a host of other electronics that become somewhat useless when there is no electricity available to sustain the operation of sundry devices. A sigh of relief is often the response when electricity is finally restored.

In Biblical times, there was no electricity but there was always illumination from the sun, moon and stars. There were special occasions where a brilliant light became visible. One occasion and experience occurs in I Kings 18. Elijah has challenged the prophets of Baal to a contest focusing on the altar of sacrifice. There had been a prolonged time of severe drought throughout the land. The "blame game" was employed in Elijah's day even as it is in ours – never accept responsibility of one's actions when it is more convenient to blame someone else. The summation of the issue is In verses 16 through 18 (NLT) – when Ahab and Elijah meet – "Obadiah went to tell Ahab that Elijah had come, and Ahab went out to meet him. So it's you, is it -- Israel's troublemaker? Ahab asked when he saw him. I have made no trouble for Israel, Elijah replied. You and your family are the troublemakers, for you have refused to obey the commands of the Lord and have worshiped the images of Baal instead..." Obviously, someone is in error here – both assertions cannot be true. Elijah seizes on the moment and tells Ahab in verses 19-20 – "Now bring all the people of Israel to Mount Carmel, with all 450 prophets of Baal and the 400 prophets of Asherah, who are supported by Jezebel. So Ahab summoned all the people and the prophets to Mount Carmel...."

From this point onward, Elijah takes control of this event and establishes the parameters for a contest with the prophets of Baal. There is one other matter Elijah decides upon before the contest begins, namely, where are the people in their relationship with the Lord. In other words, who do they acknowledge as Lord in terms of their country and their lives. Elijah inquires in verse 21 – "Then Elijah stood in front of them and said, How long are you going to waver between two opinions? If the Lord is God, follow him! But if Baal is God, then follow him! But the people were completely silent." Can you begin to imagine the extent of that silence? The Message Translation states the key phrase: "Make up your minds! Nobody said a word; nobody made a move." The NKJV translates the phrase: "But the people answered him not a word." No utterance and no sound of any kind. They were completely and totally mute. What a chilling and sad moment – an opportunity to assert one's faith and confidence in the Lord and taking a stand with one of the Lord's prophets – but – not a sound and no movement of any kind.

Elijah may have been disappointed in the response of the Lord's people but he was undaunted in terms of what he knew he could prove – namely – that the Lord is God of gods; Lord of lords and King of kings! The people weren't sure whereas Elijah was absolutely persuaded. It's the same type of personal testimony embraced by the Apostle Paul in Romans 8:38-39, "For I am persuaded that neither death nor life, nor angels nor principalities nor powers, nor things present nor things to come, nor height nor depth, nor any other created thing, shall be able to separate us from the love of God which is in Christ Jesus our Lord." Elijah was likewise persuaded in terms of God's omnipotence – power – and it could not be and would not be thwarted by any man's best effort. The challenge is set before the prophets of Baal – see if your god will respond and consume the sacrifice that is on the altar. They try and work themselves to a near frenzy as Elijah chides them and ridicules their god (verse 27) – "Shout louder! he said. Surely he is a god! Perhaps he is deep in thought, or busy, or traveling. Maybe he is sleeping and must be awakened." The result of all their effort (verse 29) – "Midday passed, and they continued their frantic prophesying until the time for the evening sacrifice. But there was no response, no one answered, no one paid attention."

The time has arrived for Elijah to put an end to this farce being perpetrated by the prophets of Baal. A subtle but important action is taken by Elijah – the people who had been silent are now directed to be involved in the building of an altar to the Lord. It is also used as a time to remind them of their heritage and history. Note verses 30-35, "Then Elijah said to all the people, Come here to me. They came to him, and he repaired the altar of the Lord, which was in ruins. Elijah took twelve stones, one for each of the tribes descended from Jacob, to whom the word of the Lord had come, saying, Your name shall be Israel. With the stones he built an altar in the name of the Lord, and he dug a trench around it large enough to hold two seahs (in land measurement, a space of 50 cubits long and 50 cubits broad; a seah is a little more than a peck)) of seed. He arranged the wood, cut the bull into pieces and laid it on the wood. Then he said to them, Fill four large jars with water and pour it on the offering and on the wood. Do it again, he said, and they did it again. Do it a third time, he ordered, and they did it the third time. The water ran down around the altar and even filled the trench."

From this point forward, there will be no mistaking who is in control and who is to be acknowledged. It will be clearly established that it is all about God and not about man. It will be demonstrated that God works through a man to will and to do of His good pleasure. Elijah approaches the Lord with absolute certainty and in verses 36-38, we read: "...at the time of the offering of the oblation, Elijah the prophet came near and said, O Lord, God of Abraham, Isaac, and Israel, let it be known this day that you are God in Israel, and that I am your servant, and that I have done all these things at your word. Answer me, O Lord, answer me, that this people may know that you, O Lord, are God, and that you have turned their hearts back. Then the fire of the Lord fell and consumed the burnt offering and the wood and the stones and the dust, and licked up the water that was in the trench."

The entire event has a twofold purpose: (1) to demonstrate the error of the prophets of Baal – their religion is a mere form and is absent of any meaningful content; and (2) to call an erring people to return to the Living Lord, Who alone has power to save and deliver to the uttermost (a youth evangelist used to say – God will save from the gutter-most to the utter-most).

The fire comes down from heaven! It is bright/brilliant and possesses fervent heat. It consumes not only the sacrifice, but laps up the water and leaves the altar in ashes. When the people see this with their own eyes and experience this display of the power and presence of God on Mount Carmel, they spontaneously respond – verses 39: "...when all the people saw it, they fell on their faces and said, The Lord, he is God; the Lord, he is God." Then Elijah calls upon them to confirm what they are now saying. It is a call to action - verse 40 – "...Elijah said to them, Seize the prophets of Baal; let not one of them escape. And they seized them. And Elijah brought them down to the brook Kishon and slaughtered them there." The brilliant light – the consuming fire from heaven – brought the people to a point of realization that they had departed from the Lord and needed to return to Him. Another aspect to this is that if they persisted in rebellion and sin, they would also be subjected to the judgment and power of God.

Another situation where the brilliant light is a factor is shared in Acts 9:1-9. It is a dramatic and impressive moment. Paul is at his zenith – a very high point – in his obsession to persecute the Church of Jesus Christ. The text states the extent of the persecution and the impact of this moment – "But Saul, still breathing threats and murder against the disciples of the Lord, went to the high priest and asked him for letters to the synagogues at Damascus, so that if he found any belonging to the Way, men or women, he might bring them bound to Jerusalem. Now as he went on his way, he approached Damascus, and suddenly a light from heaven flashed around him. And falling to the ground he heard a voice saying to him, Saul, Saul, why are you persecuting me? And he said, Who are you, Lord? And he said, I am Jesus, whom you are persecuting. But rise and enter the city, and you will be told what you are to do. The men who were traveling with him stood speechless, hearing the voice but seeing no one. Saul rose from the ground, and although his eyes were opened, he saw nothing. So they led him by the hand and brought him into Damascus. And for three days he was without sight, and neither ate nor drank…" The Lord intervenes and slams on the brakes of this persecution express. He does so in a very dramatic way – a brilliant light – and it strikes Saul and stops him instantaneously. This one who has been "breathing threats and murder against the disciples of the Lord" is now – (a) stopped in his tracks; (b) is helpless on the ground; (c) is scared and not knowing what will happen next; (d) is humbled – others have to lead him by the hand into Damascus; (e) cannot see for three days; and (f) neither eats nor drinks for the same length of days.

Can you begin to imagine what the people in Damascus thought as they saw and heard what had occurred with Saul – that the persecutor has been confronted by the Lord Jesus

Christ? Is this something they would or could believe? What if you had been in Damascus, would you have believed it? There is a sense of what your response might've been when in verses 10-15, Ananias is called upon to interact with Saul of Tarsus. Note the words – "Now there was a disciple at Damascus named Ananias. The Lord said to him in a vision, Ananias. And he said, Here I am, Lord. And the Lord said to him, Rise and go to the street called Straight, and at the house of Judas look for a man of Tarsus named Saul, for behold, he is praying, and he has seen in a vision a man named Ananias come in and lay his hands on him so that he might regain his sight. But Ananias answered, Lord, I have heard from many about this man, how much evil he has done to your saints at Jerusalem. And here he has authority from the chief priests to bind all who call on your name. But the Lord said to him, Go, for he is a chosen instrument of mine to carry my name before the Gentiles and kings and the children of Israel." Ananias talks to the Lord about the normal fear of all the people because they had heard about the authority Saul had from the Chief Priests and knew of the action that Saul was very willing to carry out against the Lord's people.

With all of his apprehension... fear... trepidation – Ananias goes in the name of the Lord. An old saying – "the proof of the pudding is in the tasting" – is about to become the reality for Ananias and the people in Jerusalem. In verses 17-22 – "... Ananias departed and entered the house. And laying his hands on him he said, Brother Saul, the Lord Jesus who appeared to you on the road by which you came has sent me so that you may regain your sight and be filled with the Holy Spirit. And immediately something like scales fell from his eyes, and he regained his sight. Then he rose and was baptized; and taking food, he was strengthened. For some days he was with the disciples at Damascus. And immediately he proclaimed Jesus in the synagogues, saying, He is the Son of God. And all who heard him were amazed and said, Is not this the man who made havoc in Jerusalem of those who called upon this name? And has he not come here for this purpose, to bring them bound before the chief priests? But Saul increased all the more in strength, and confounded the Jews who lived in Damascus by proving that Jesus was the Christ." The brilliant light from heaven stopped a man who was obsessed with the purposes of darkness but is now converted and transformed as he tells people about the only true Light – Jesus Christ. Saul is now calling people who are bound in the darkness of sin to follow the One Who will set them free – Jesus Christ – and give them the privilege to implement into their lives I John 1:7 – "...if we walk in the light, as he is in the light, we have fellowship with one another, and the blood of Jesus his Son cleanses us from all sin." Philip P. Bliss captured this thought when he penned a Hymn in 1875, The Light Of The World Is Jesus - - -

The whole world was lost In the darkness of sin,
The Light of the world is Jesus!
Like sunshine at noonday, His glory shone in.
The Light of the world is Jesus!
Refrain
Come to the light, 'tis shining for thee;
Sweetly the light has dawned upon me.
Once I was blind, but now I can see:
The Light of the world is Jesus!

No darkness have we Who in Jesus abide;
The Light of the world is Jesus!
We walk in the light When we follow our Guide!
The Light of the world is Jesus!

The third illustration of the brilliant light is given in Mark 9:2-13. A description of what Peter, James and John are seeing is given in verses 2-3 – "And after six days Jesus took with him Peter and James and John, and led them up a high mountain by themselves. And he was transfigured before them, and his clothes became radiant, intensely white, as no one on earth could bleach them." A bright and brilliant light from heaven brought about this moment. Just as suddenly, in verse 4 – "...there appeared to them Elijah with Moses, and they were talking with Jesus..." The one who would represent the prophets and the one who represented the Law from God – both of them having experienced a miraculous death and departure from the earth – now miraculously stand and converse with Jesus Christ (Who Himself will miraculously depart from the earth at The Ascension).

There are times and moments when silence is golden – a time when nothing should be said – just listen and observe. But this behavior is contrary to the nature of Peter, and we read in verses 5-6 – "Peter said to Jesus, Rabbi, it is good that we are here. Let us make three tents, one for you and one for Moses and one for Elijah. For he did not know what to say, for they were terrified." Peter's idea was to build three monuments to these three men – a tent (tabernacle) for Elijah, and one for Moses, and one for Jesus Christ. Peter should've succumbed to his being terrified and "he did not know what to say" posture. It is allowed that Peter must've had very clean feet because every time he opened his mouth – he put one of his feet into it. In verses 7-8, there are three significant statements given to Peter, James and John – "...a cloud overshadowed them, and a voice came out of the cloud, This is my beloved Son; listen to him. And suddenly, looking around, they no longer saw anyone with them but Jesus only." The voice from the cloud – God, the

Father – states these three things very plainly: (1) This is My Beloved Son; (2) Listen to Him; and (3) it is Jesus only – "looking around, they no longer saw anyone with them but Jesus only."

If only these words from God, the Father could be grasped by each and every follower of Jesus Christ, namely, (1) recognize who he is – the Beloved Son of God (John 3:16); and (2) we are to listen to Him at all times and about all things – obeying His instruction to us; and (3) we are to be completely focused upon Jesus Only (Hebrews 12:1-2) and not distracted by the noise or things of the world. Jesus alone is the Brilliant Light sent from God who has penetrated the darkness of this world and men's hearts (John 1:9-13). We are expected to implement at all times and in all places the words of Jesus – the Brilliant Light – Who said – Matthew 5:14-16 - "You are the light of the world. A city set on a hill cannot be hidden. Nor do people light a lamp and put it under a basket, but on a stand, and it gives light to all in the house. In the same way, let your light shine before others, so that they may see your good works and give glory to your Father who is in heaven."

Be willing to be one of the bright lights that is shining in the midst of darkness. Let us never be ashamed to be identified with the Brilliant Light – Jesus Christ – but let us represent Him boldly and honorably. When we are Taking A Serious God Seriously, a chorus we taught our children was can be the ongoing song of our lives - - -

This Little Light of Mine – I'm gonna let it shine,
Let it shine…!

Hide it under a bushel? No! – I'm gonna let it shine.
Let it shine…!

**Don't let Satan blow it out – I'm gonna let it shine.
Let it shine…!**

**Let it shine 'til Jesus comes – I'm gonna let it shine.
Let it shine…!**

QUESTIONS FOR THOUGHT AND APPLICATION

1.   In the lifetime of most, the most brilliant light one encounters would be a lightning strike. Lightning is very powerful as
well as being exceedingly brilliant. If one is struck by a bolt of
lightning it can result in death or bodily harm. In Psalm 77:18,
when contemplating this display of God's power, how does the
Psalmist describe its appearance and its effect?

What does walking in God's light indicate one is knowing and
experiencing?

2.   Acts 9:1-9 indicates another situation where and when the
brilliant light from heaven becomes an important and major
factor. The one experiencing the effects of this brilliant light is
Saul of Tarsus. Why was Saul singled out for this encounter and
experience? What had he been doing?

As he was approaching Damascus, a brilliant light – suddenly –
flashed around him from heaven - knocked him to the ground -
and - blinded his eyes. He also heard a voice.
What did that voice say to him?
What was the time-frame for his blindness?
Did Saul know who the voice belonged to at that point?
What did he do to determine who was speaking to him?
What response did he receive?

3.   Another instance and display of the brilliant light from
heaven is recorded in Mark 9:2-13. Jesus took Peter, James and
John with Him up to a high mountain. It is at this point that the
bright light illuminates that area.
In addition to the brilliant light, what else transpired on the
mountain? Who suddenly appeared with Jesus?

What was represented by those who appeared alongside of Jesus on that occasion?
What was the response of Peter, James and John when they saw what occurred?
There is an interesting sentence in Vs. 6. How does Mark report that moment in time? What does he say happened, and what was the condition of the three disciples?

4.   In Matthew 24:23-27, Jesus responds to the disciples' interest in His coming again. Jesus makes reference to lightning. What does He mean when he says: "For as the lightning comes from the east and flashes to the west, so also will the coming of the Son of Man be."
What does his use of "lightning" indicate? Can one calculate when or where the lightning will appear? When Jesus does return, will His appearance be confined to a geographical area or will all be able to see and know His appearance?

5.   In Revelation 18:21-24, something will occur in Babylon.

6.   In Vs. 23, what is the judgment that will occur? What will shine no more?

7.   In Revelation 21:22-24, what will be the only light available? Who is The Source of that Light?

8.   In terms of the Light Source in Revelation 21, is it similar to or the same as that which is stated in Psalm 19:1? Explain.

Jesus said to the people, "I am the light of the world.
If you follow me, you won't be stumbling through the darkness, because you will have the light that leads to life."
                                                    John 8:12 (NLT)

When Light Fails to Light

"...keep your father's commandment, and forsake not your mother's teaching. Bind them on your heart always; tie them around your neck. When you walk, they will lead you; when you lie down, they will watch over you; and when you awake, they will talk with you. For the commandment is a lamp and the teaching a light, and the reproofs of discipline are the way of life..." Proverbs 6:20-23

D.L. Moody gave this account:

On a dark, stormy, night, when the waves rolled like mountains, and not a star was to be seen, a boat, rocking and plunging, neared the Cleveland harbor. "Are you sure this is Cleveland?" asked the captain, seeing only one light from the lighthouse.

"Quite sure, sir," replied the pilot.

"Where are the lower lights?"

"Gone out, sir."

"Can you make the harbor?"

"We must, or perish, sir!"

And with a strong hand and a brave heart, the old pilot turned the wheel. But alas, in the darkness he missed the channel, and with a crash upon the rocks the boat was shivered, and many a life lost in a watery grave. Brethren, the Master will take care of the great light-house: let us keep the lower lights burning!

Those words became an inspiration for a Hymn written by Philip P. Bliss in 1871 entitled and utilized over the years by many Rescue Missions: Let The Lower Lights Be Burning - - -

Brightly beams our Father's mercy

from His lighthouse evermore,
But to us He gives to us the keeping
of the lights along the shore.
Let the lower lights be burning!
Send a gleam across the wave!
For to us He gives the keeping of the lights along the shore.

Dark the night of sin has settled,
loud the angry billows roar;
Eager eyes are watching, longing,
for the lights, along the shore.
Let the lower lights be burning!
Send a gleam across the wave!
Eager eyes are watching, longing,
for the lights, along the shore.

Trim your feeble lamp, my brother,
some poor soul is tempest tossed,
Trying now to make the harbor,
in the darkness may be lost.
Let the lower lights be burning!
Send a gleam across the wave!
Trying now to make the harbor,
some poor soul who may be lost.

What happens when a light fails to give light? There is nothing wrong with the source (electricity); nothing is wrong with the lamp; and nothing is wrong with the bulb – all have been tested and found to be functional. Is it possible that the one who possesses the lamp has failed to plug it into the source that will result in the benefit of the light shining and illuminating in the darkness?

Jesus was concerned that His followers had awareness regarding the dangers of the darkness. Immediately after His statement in John 3:16 – the Gospel in a nutshell – Jesus shared this thought and teaching in John 3:18-21 – "Whoever believes in him is not condemned, but whoever does not believe is condemned already, because he has not believed in the name of the only Son of God. And this is the judgment: the light has come into the world, and people loved the darkness rather than the light because their works were evil. For everyone who does wicked things hates the light and does not come to the light, lest his works should be exposed. But whoever does what is true comes to the light, so that it may be clearly seen that his works have been carried out in God." Jesus was mindful of the human propensity to be attracted to the things of darkness. He clearly stated the difference and contrast between Light and Darkness and shows there can be no embracing of both – either one has committed his/her life to the Path of Light – or remains content with the innate desire to walk in the Path of Darkness. It is obvious that Jesus is teaching that one must make a choice between the two – walking in the Light or walking in the Darkness.

On one occasion while giving the Sermon on the Mount Jesus made this principle very clear when he stated – Matthew 6:24 – "No one can serve two masters, for either he will hate the one and love the other, or he will be devoted to the one and despise the other. You cannot serve God and money." The Apostle Paul would express this same principle in a series of questions he asked in II Corinthians 6:14-16 when he was focusing on how each believer is a Temple of the Living God – "Do not be unequally yoked with unbelievers. For what partnership has righteousness with lawlessness? Or what fellowship has light with darkness? What accord has Christ with

Belial? Or what portion does a believer share with an unbeliev-er? What agreement has the temple of God with idols? For we are the temple of the living God; as God said, I will make my dwelling among them and walk among them, and I will be their God, and they shall be my people." In other words, the Word of the Lord is that Light. It underscores that Light and Darkness are incompatible with each other. Where Light is present, the Darkness must be – will be - penetrated and expelled.

Some feel they have a lot of time to make a commitment to Jesus Christ, and they choose to straddle the proverbial fence – and they find out they have wasted too many years and are too late to come to the Light. It is similar to those who ignored the message of Noah in Genesis 6-9 – until the rain started to fall – then in panic they ran toward the door of the Ark – but – they were too late because God had closed and sealed the door. Jesus indicated this truth in John 12:35-36 when He gave this appeal – "So Jesus said to them, The light is among you for a little while longer. Walk while you have the light, lest darkness overtake you. The one who walks in the darkness does not know where he is going. While you have the light, believe in the light, that you may become sons of light."

A primary custodian of the message regarding the Light, is the Church. The special duty and responsibility for that custodi-al care rests in the leadership of the particular Church. The Book of Acts demonstrates that as the Gospel was proclaimed, and as people responded to that message, they were added to The Church. Most of the New Testament is written to the various churches that had been formed in cities where the Apostles travelled and preached. There is a very compelling review of these churches given in Revelation 1 through 3. The general idea is that the Head of The Church is coming to the various churches. The introductory words of The Apostle John state in Revelation 1:4-8, "John to the seven churches that are in Asia: Grace to you and peace from him who is and who was and who is to come, and from the seven spirits who are before his throne, and from Jesus Christ the faithful witness, the firstborn of the dead, and the ruler of kings on earth. To him who loves us and has freed us from our sins by his blood and made us a kingdom, priests to his God and Father, to him be glory and dominion forever and ever. Amen. Behold, he is coming with the clouds, and every eye will see him, even those who pierced him, and all tribes of the earth will wail on account of him. Even so. Amen. I am the Alpha and the Omega, says the Lord God, who is and who was and who is to come, the Almighty." In His time and by His choice, He will come to His Church. What will He find when He comes? What will His Church be doing? Will they be carrying out the Biblical mandates or a program of a church growth movement? What message will He hear proclaimed – the message of the Gospel and repentance or one that will merely make people feel good about themselves?

In his vision, John suddenly sees Jesus returning. John writes what he sees and gives these defining words in Revelation 1:17-20, "When I saw him, I fell at his feet as though dead. But he laid his right hand on me, saying, Fear not, I am the first and the last, and the living one. I died, and behold I am alive forevermore, and I have the keys of Death and Hades. Write therefore the things that you have seen, those that are and those that are to take place after this. As for the mystery of the seven stars that you saw in my right hand, and the seven golden lamp-stands, the seven stars are the angels of the seven churches, and the seven lamp-stands are the seven churches." Revelation 2 and 3 is when Jesus walks in the midst of the churches. There is a prevailing threefold theme that applies to most of the Churches – (1) Remember, (2) Repent, and (3) Return. The message of Jesus to His Church is that there are noticeable discrepancies within them that must be addressed and eliminated if they are to serve the Lord efficiently and effectively. The Message of Light is precise and must always be engaged in piercing the darkness. If the church allows itself to forget its purpose and mission, then it is no longer useful and there is no rationale for why it should continue to exist. It is never to be merely a social club and/or a community center. If a survey of the churches was done by one who was measuring whether or not true worship of God was taking place in a particular Church, the result would horrify many. The estimate would be very high – maybe close to 80% - where people would not be able to verbalize what true worship is and means, not could they defend what they were doing in a church service met the requirements and standards of God for worship in His Church. Are they a Church that is maintaining a tradition or merely the status quo? Is it a place where the light is failing to be a light that shines and penetrates the darkness? Is it a Church that desperately needs to (1) Remember therefore from where you have fallen; and (2) Repent, and (3) Return to do the works you did at first?

The Lord is very precise in stipulating the primary causes for the light not shining as it should. If one is able to visualize the particular church as being a Lighthouse whose primary function is to send a penetrating beam of light over a wide expanse of water to warn the ships at sea of the dangers – reefs, rocks, sandbars, shallow water – if they drift too closely toward the shoreline. An illustration of the preciseness of the Lord regarding His people and His Church is stated in Jeremiah 23:10-14, "...the land is full of adulterers; For because of a curse the land mourns. The pleasant places of the wilderness are dried up. Their course of life is evil, And their might is not right. For both prophet and priest are profane; Yes, in My house I have found their wickedness, says the Lord. Therefore their way shall be to them Like slippery ways; In the darkness they shall be driven on And fall in them; For I will bring disaster on them, The year of their punishment, says the Lord. And I have seen folly in the prophets of Samaria: They prophesied by Baal And caused My people Israel to err. Also I have seen a horrible thing in the prophets of Jerusalem: They commit adultery and walk in lies; They also strengthen the hands of evildoers, So that no one turns back from his wickedness. All of them are like Sodom to Me, And her inhabitants like Gomorrah.´ The ones who have the obligation to proclaim the Holy Words of the Lord are not doing so – and – the Lord has taken notice of their message and practice. They have not established a moral compass in the midst of God's people and they all are on the precipice of the slippery slope.

The Lord also has a word for the Shepherds who are supposed to set a standard before the flock and lead the flock in safe and verdant pastures. The Lord observes in Jeremiah 23:1-4, "Woe to the shepherds who destroy and scatter the sheep of My pasture! says the Lord. Therefore thus says the Lord God of Israel against the shepherds who feed My people: You have scattered My flock, driven them away, and not attended to them. Behold, I will attend to you for the evil of your doings, says the Lord..." In an August 9, 2011 release by Framework Productions – Framing The Biblical Worldview, the following is stated regarding the state of the Church in much of Europe today: "Wim Lizette de Klerk says – 'Here you can believe what you want to think for yourself, what you really feel and believe is true. Clergy are story tellers and not men of God in much of

Europe. Pray for His Church to rise.'" In a report by the BBC on August 5, 2011 regarding the shift in the belief system of the Church in Holland, they report: "The Rev. Klaas Hendrikse can offer his congregation little hope of life after death, and he's not the sort of man to sugar the pill.

The Exodus Church is part of the mainstream Protestant Church in the Netherlands An imposing figure in black robes and white clerical collar, Mr. Hendrikse presides over the Sunday service at the Exodus Church in Gorinchem, central Holland. It is part of the mainstream Protestant Church in the Netherlands (PKN), and the service is conventional enough, with hymns, readings from the Bible, and the Lord's Prayer. But the message from Mr. Hendrikse's sermon seems bleak – 'Make the most of life on earth, because it will probably be the only one you get'. 'Personally I have no talent for believing in life after death,' Mr Hendrikse says. 'No, for me our life, our task, is before death.' Nor does Klaas Hendrikse believe that God exists at all as a supernatural thing."

In a similar situation, the BBC also reports that The Rev Klaas Hendrikse states: "When it happens, it happens down to earth, between you and me, between people, that's where it can happen. God is not a being at all...it's a word for experience, or human experience. Mr Hendrikse describes the Bible's account of Jesus' life as a mythological story about a man who may never have existed, even if it is a valuable source of wisdom about how to lead a good life. His book Believing in a Non-Existent God led to calls from more traditionalist Christians for him to be removed. However, a special church meeting decided his views were too widely shared among church thinkers for him to be singled out. A study by the Free University of Amsterdam found that one-in-six clergy in the PKN and six other smaller denominations was either agnostic or atheist."

Other comments made by some Dutch Clergy include: Klaas Hendrikse: "You don't have to believe that Jesus was physically resurrected" The Rev Kirsten Slettenaar, Exodus Church's regular priest, also rejects the idea - widely considered central to Christianity - that Jesus was divine as well as human. "I think 'Son of God' is a kind of title," she says. "I don't think he was a god or a half god. I think he was a man, but he was a special man because he was very good in living from out of love, from out of the spirit of God he found inside himself." Mrs. Slettenaar acknowledges that she's changing what the Church has said, but, she insists, not the "real meaning of Christianity". She says that there "is not only one answer" and complains that "a lot of traditional beliefs are outside people and have grown into rigid things that you can't touch any more". Dienie van Wijngaarden, who's been going to Exodus Church for 20 years, is among lay people attracted to such free thinking. Some believe that traditional Christianity has too restrictive a notion of the nature of God "I think it's very liberating. Klaas Hendrikse is using the Bible in a metaphorical way so I can bring it to my own way of thinking, my own way of doing." Wim De Jong says, "Here you can believe what you want to think for yourself, what you really feel and believe is true." Professor Hijme Stoffels of the VU University Amsterdam says…"In our society it's called 'somethingism'." There must be 'something' between heaven and earth, but to call it 'God', and even 'a personal God', for the majority of Dutch is a bridge too far. Christian churches are in a market situation. They can offer their ideas to a majority of the population which is interested in spirituality or some kind of religion. To compete in this market of ideas, some Christian groups seem ready virtually to reinvent Christianity. They want the Netherlands to be a laboratory for Christianity, experimenting with radical new ways of understanding the faith."

In these and other instances, the light has been dimmed and is almost completely extinguished. They have chosen to ignore the dangers and have diluted the warnings that should be sent out in the name of the Lord. Despite their failure and refusal to be a true messenger of God, the Lord is neither frustrated nor denied in terms of His eternal plan and purpose. When He is rebuking and rejecting the work and ethic of the shepherds, prophets and priests, He declares what He will do (Jeremiah 23): "But I will gather the remnant of My flock out of all countries where I have driven them, and bring them back to their folds; and they shall be fruitful and increase. I will set up shepherds over them who will feed them; and they shall fear no more, nor be dismayed, nor shall they be lacking, says the Lord."

The shepherds, prophets and priest have not faithfully carried out their ministry call from God. They have allowed for gross negligence of God's Word and sacrifices; they have allowed behavior that is contrary to God's Law and Standards; they have not offered a word of correction or issued a call for Holy and Righteous living. The light of God's Word has been dimmed to accommodate the pressures of the culture and the preferences of the flock. They have forgotten to keep God and His Word central before the people! The message of – repent and be converted – has long been ignored. One is reminded of the message of the Resurrection declared by the Apostle Paul in I Corinthians 15:13-20, "...if there is no resurrection of the dead, then Christ is not risen. And if Christ is not risen, then our preaching is empty and your faith is also empty. Yes, and we are found false witnesses of God, because we have testified of God that He raised up Christ, whom He did not raise up--if in fact the dead do not rise. For if the dead do not rise, then Christ is not risen. And if Christ is not risen, your faith is futile; you are still in your sins! Then also those who have fallen asleep in Christ have perished. If in this life only we have hope in Christ, we are of all men the most pitiable. But now Christ is risen from the dead, and has become the first-fruits of those who have fallen asleep." Take note of verse 19, "If in this life only we have hope in Christ, we are of all men the most pitiable." The previous statements by Dutch and European Clergy are clearly stating that which is in contradiction to the Holy Scriptures. The Message Translation of these verses is: "If there's no resurrection, there's no living Christ. And face it - if there's no resurrection for Christ, everything we've told you is smoke and mirrors, and everything you've staked your life on is smoke and mirrors. Not only that, but we would be guilty of telling a string of barefaced lies about God, all these affidavits we passed on to you verifying that God raised up Christ - sheer fabrications, if there's no resurrection. If corpses can't be raised, then Christ wasn't, because he was indeed dead. And if Christ wasn't raised, then all you're doing is wandering about in the dark, as lost as ever. It's even worse for those who died hoping in Christ and resurrection, because they're already in their graves. If all we get out of Christ is a little inspiration for a few short years, we're a pretty sorry lot. But the truth is that Christ has been raised up, the first in a long legacy of those who are going to leave the cemeteries." Those who identify with the theories and false teaching of the churches in Europe and the Netherlands would do well to read and reread theses verses in The Message Translation where the Resurrection of Jesus Christ is stated clearly, succinctly and unequivocally.

Just these summary words in II Timothy 3:12-17, where we can contrast the malaise that is creeping into the midst of the shepherds, prophets and priests – and – that which is contained in the mandate regarding God's Word. Paul wrote to

Timothy: "Yes, and all who desire to live godly in Christ Jesus will suffer persecution. But evil men and impostors will grow worse and worse, deceiving and being deceived. But you must continue in the things which you have learned and been assured of, knowing from whom you have learned them, and that from childhood you have known the Holy Scriptures, which are able to make you wise for salvation through faith which is in Christ Jesus. All Scripture is given by inspiration of God, and is profitable for doctrine, for reproof, for correction, for instruction in righteousness, that the man of God may be complete, thoroughly equipped for every good work." What should you believe and champion – the approach unfolding in Europe and the Netherlands – or the time-tested message of the Word of God. The real measure of the professing "Christian" and the one who claims to be following God and His word is – How often do you find yourself making accommodation with the world, and allowing for compromises so that other's feelings won't be hurt? How often do you look the other way and remain silent when you ought to face situations and individuals head-on and speak the word of Truth from the Book of Truth – God's Word? Do you remain silent when that which is false is being proclaimed and practiced because you were reared to be "nice" and to be "respectful" rather than confrontational?

We need to remember and implement frequently the words of Ephesians 6:10-13 – "...be strong in the Lord and in the strength of his might. Put on the whole armor of God, that you may be able to stand against the schemes of the devil. For we do not wrestle against flesh and blood, but against the rulers, against the authorities, against the cosmic powers over this present darkness, against the spiritual forces of evil in the heavenly places. Therefore take up the whole armor of God, that you may be able to withstand in the evil day, and having done all, to stand firm." The thrust of these verses is that one is to (a) be strong in the Lord" and (b) and having done all, to stand firm. The New Living Translations states these verses: "A final word: Be strong with the Lord's mighty power. Put on all of God's armor so that you will be able to stand firm against all strategies and tricks of the Devil. For we are not fighting against people made of flesh and blood, but against the evil rulers and authorities of the unseen world, against those mighty powers of darkness who rule this world, and against wicked spirits in the heavenly realms. Use every piece of God's armor to resist the enemy in the time of evil, so that after the battle you will still be standing firm." These are the marching orders for the child of God. Anything less than this represents compromise, cowardice, accommodation with wickedness, and a lack of solid conviction in terms of (a) Who God is, and (b) How God requires you to live.

The words of an old Hymn are inspiring and challenging for all of us in these days. It was written in 1885 and is entitled: The Banner of The Cross - - -

There's a royal banner given for display
To the soldiers of the King;
As an ensign fair we lift it up today,
While as ransomed ones we sing.

Though the foe may rage and gather as the flood,
Let the standard be displayed;
And beneath its folds, as soldiers of the Lord,
For the truth be not dismayed!
Refrain
Marching on, marching on,
For Christ count everything but loss!

And to crown Him King, we'll toil and sing,
'Neath the banner of the cross!

This is a serious challenge for one to do a serious and risky task, namely, to be engaged in the battle for the souls of mankind. There is no room or time for spectators any longer. The battle lines are drawn and the enemy is fully engaged. Any lingering or inordinate delay only gives the enemy greater opportunity to gain inroads. When that infiltration occurs, there can be considerable undermining of the cause in which we are to be seriously and fully engaged. Some of Paul's epistles close with a warning to beware of those within a group who are actually on the enemy's side. An example is given in II Timothy 2:16-21, "But avoid irreverent babble, for it will lead people into more and more ungodliness, and their talk will spread like gangrene. Among them are Hymenaeus and Philetus, who have swerved from the truth, saying that the resurrection has already happened. They are upsetting the faith of some. But God's firm foundation stands, bearing this seal: The Lord knows those who are His, and, Let everyone who names the name of the Lord depart from iniquity. Now in a great house there are not only vessels of gold and silver but also of wood and clay, some for honorable use, some for dishonorable. Therefore, if anyone cleanses himself from what is dishonorable, he will be a vessel for honorable use, set apart as holy, useful to the master of the house, ready for every good work."

There is never a time or place for accepting those who embrace error and impact the body. It is a disease that requires treatment and remedy. The one promoting error must be identified and removed otherwise the entire "church" will become affected. The enemy will have gained the victory from within. These are serious times. If the people of God understand that He is serious all of the time, then the true Church should be in serious lock-step with Him! The only question one must answer at this point is whether or not one is in a serious relationship with a very serious God! Are you?

QUESTIONS FOR THOUGHT AND APPLICATION

1.   When one builds a home and is ready to occupy it, what is a major preparation one must make regarding the utilities for the house?

2.   Upon moving into the home and placing the furniture in the rooms, what if none of the electrical fixtures is plugged into any of the power outlets, will any of them work as they are designed to do?

Where is the failure in terms of getting lamps to light, etc.? Is it the power source or one's failure to plug into the power source that is available?

3.   In Matthew 28:18-20, when Jesus states that "All authority is given unto Me...Go...", what is that authority? What does the "authority" of Jesus represent?

4.   Is the "authority" of Jesus present and represented in Acts 1:8, when Jesus says: "But you shall receive power when the Holy Spirit has come upon you; and you shall be witnesses to Me in Jerusalem, and in all Judea and Samaria, and to the end of the earth."?

5.   What if an individual or church fails to place itself under the authority of Jesus Christ, will that person or church be a light that fails to light? Why?

6.   Suppose that same individual or church plugs into the power source in Acts 1:8, will that person or church be a light that not only lights but also serves as a beacon for those who are mired in the darkness? Why?

7.   Once a person has submitted to the Authority of Jesus Christ and is empowered by the Holy Spirit he/she is positioned to do and accomplish exploits for God. What is an exploit? Can you cite any examples from Scripture of those who accomplished exploits for God? (Hints: Look in the Book of Daniel and in The Book of Acts - Daniel 1:8, Daniel 3, Daniel 6, Acts 15:25-26).

8.   These were ordinary men who God saw fit to use in extraordinary ways. Is God able to do the same with ordinary people today? What must be characteristic and unique about the person or church God will use to accomplish exploits for Him?

(a)   Individually, what must they have done in terms of Christ's Authority?
(b)   Individually, what must they have done in terms of Spirit Empowerment?

9.   When Jesus walked in the midst of the seven churches (Revelation 2 and 3), there is a common thread and theme with each church, namely, Remember, Repent and Return. There is an obvious application for the church today. Following that thread and theme - -

(a)   What must one REMEMBER?
(b)   Of what must one REPENT?
(c)   To what must one RETURN?

10. Three more "R" words are present in Psalm 85:4-6 when the Psalmist prays: "RESTORE us, O God of our salvation, And cause Your anger toward us to cease. Will You be angry with us

forever? Will You prolong Your anger to all generations? Will You not REVIVE us again, That Your people may REJOICE in You? Show us Your mercy, Lord, And grant us Your salvation." Do you see these "R's" present in the "church" you attend? Why?

(a)   What would be involved in the RESTORE process for an individual or church today?

(b)   What is entailed in an individual or church in the REVIVE event or process today?

(c)   What is the most legitimate cause and purpose for the REJOICE factor to be present?

Be diligent to present yourself approved to God,
a worker who does not need to be ashamed...
Nevertheless the solid foundation of God stands, having this
seal: "The Lord knows those who are His," and,
"Let everyone who names the name of Christ depart from
iniquity..."
            II Timothy 2:15-21 (NKJV – Selected)

Malfunction and Correction

"And you were dead in the trespasses and sins in which you once walked, following the course of this world, following the prince of the power of the air, the spirit that is now at work in the sons of disobedience-- among whom we all once lived in the passions of our flesh, carrying out the desires of the body and the mind, and were by nature children of wrath, like the rest of mankind." Ephesians 2:1-3

"Therefore remember that at one time you Gentiles in the flesh, called the uncircumcision by what is called the circumcision, which is made in the flesh by hands-- remember that you were at that time separated from Christ, alienated from the commonwealth of Israel and strangers to the covenants of promise, having no hope and without God in the world." Ephesians 2: 2:11-12

One area that puzzles most people is electricity. We all know that it works but many don't know "How" it works. A simple effort to assist us in our understanding is that "Electric current is a flow of electric charge through a medium. This charge is typically carried by moving electrons in a conductor such as wire." Most of us have had some experience with the use of Fuses and Circuit Breakers – the benefit of which is to prevent an overload on a circuit or a short circuit - and to prevent any danger – such as, fire – from occurring. While we may not completely understand the "how" of electricity, we are grateful to have it and for the safeguards that are in place that should alleviate any danger or harm taking place.

The previous chapter noted that a malfunction has occurred within the "Church" and it has been made know by the Head of The Church – Jesus Christ. He is pointing out that Darkness is beginning to appear where Light is to be always present. One of the features of darkness is that it allows one to think or suppose that he can be engaged in negative behavioral matters where it won't be readily seen or noticed. It continues to echo the words of Jesus Christ (John 3:18-20 - NLT) – "But those who do not trust him have already been judged for not believing in the only Son of God. Their judgment is based on this fact: The light from heaven came into the world, but they loved the darkness more than the light, for their actions were evil. They hate the light because they want to sin in the darkness. They stay away from the light for fear their sins will be exposed and they will be punished." As wrong and as tragic as this behavior and choice is, Jesus is making the issue very clear and plain – light and darkness are contrary to one another – and – those who gravitate toward the darkness do so because their goal and ambition is to do what is evil, wrong and sinful. They have and are detaching themselves from the Light. They have weighed the two and decided that they prefer and enjoy the things that darkness offers. While doing so, they have neglected to realize that Jesus Christ has been observing them and has weighed them in His balances – and they have come up wanting.

This is very similar to the scene in Daniel 5.1-4 that informs us of what is taking place – "King Belshazzar made a great feast for a thousand of his lords and drank wine in front of the thousand. Belshazzar, when he tasted the wine, commanded that the vessels of gold and of silver that Nebuchadnezzar his father had taken out of the temple in Jerusalem be brought, that the king and his lords, his wives, and his concubines might drink from them. Then they brought in the golden vessels that had been taken out of the temple, the house of God in Jerusalem, and the king and his lords, his wives, and his concubines drank from them. They drank wine and praised the gods of gold and silver, bronze, iron, wood, and stone…" It was a festive occasion and one thing was leading to another – but – so what? No one cared and no one was in disagreement with the drunken party.

But suddenly – Daniel 5:5-6 – the festivity became a scene of fear – "Immediately the fingers of a human hand appeared and wrote on the plaster of the wall of the king's palace, opposite the lamp-stand. And the king saw the hand as it wrote. Then the king's color changed, and his thoughts alarmed him; his limbs gave way, and his knees knocked together…" No one knew what it meant – but – it could not be denied – every one in the room was cognizant of what had taken place. The party stopped and the preoccupation with the writing on the wall was now the focus. After all the wise men of the kingdom have looked at the inscription and were unable to decipher or interpret it, someone suggests that the king should send for Daniel. When Daniel arrives, in addition to his references to what had happened to his father – Nebuchadnezzar – he proceeds to the writing on the wall – Daniel 5:16-28 – "I have heard that you can give interpretations and solve problems. Now if you can read the writing and make known to me its interpretation, you shall be clothed with purple and have a chain of gold around your neck and shall be the third ruler in the kingdom. Then Daniel answered and said before the king, Let your gifts be for yourself, and give your rewards to another. Nevertheless, I will read the writing to the king and make known to him the interpretation…you have not humbled your heart… but you have lifted up yourself against the Lord of heaven. And the vessels of his house have been brought in before you, and you and your lords, your wives, and your concubines have drunk wine from them. And you have praised the gods of silver and gold, of bronze, iron, wood, and stone, which do not see or hear or know, but the God in whose hand is your breath…you have not honored. Then from His presence the hand was sent, and this writing was inscribed…MENE, MENE, TEKEL, and PARSIN. This is the interpretation of the matter: (1) God has numbered the days of your kingdom and brought it to an end; (2) you have been weighed in the balances and found wanting; (3) your kingdom is divided and given to the Medes and Persians."

The piercing words from God Himself – "weighed in the balances and found wanting"! In just as dramatic and visible manner, John sees in his vision he sees one "like the Son of Man" walking in the midst of seven lamp-stands." As John sees and hears and writes, he is told – Revelation 1:20 – "As for the mystery of the seven stars that you saw in my right hand, and the seven golden lamp-stands, the seven stars are the angels of the seven churches, and the seven lamp-stands are the seven churches." In Revelation 2 and 3, John is writing about the Churches and the Balances of God. Each of the seven Churches is going to learn which way God's Balances are tipping and what it means to be weighed by and with God's scales. They will learn whether or not there is a possibility of a "current malfunction" in their respective Church and what "correction" is required to return the Church to its true function. One of the truths to be recognized is that just as the vision of John on the Isle of Patmos represented the Lord Jesus Christ walking in the midst of the churches, that same reality is true today. And the penetrating words of Jesus written by John are just as valid for us today: "I know…"

Regardless of how the "church" today would present itself in an effort to be more appealing to the community, the One Who looks down from His heaven is saying – but – "I Know" – and "your representations must be verifiably consistent with My Standard for My people and My Church." It is a basic, vital and serious matter. The "church" may be able to fool fellow-man in the community and culture - but it cannot fool God – He "knows"!

What major truth has the "church" drifted away from and forgotten? In one's individual life, what have the pressures and duties of life been allowed to crowd out of one's spiritual focus and commitment? If one is to implement the formulation of Revelation 1 – Remember, Repent, Return – what is one to remember, repent of and return to? What is the remedy for the "church" and individual life? Is The Book of Revelation too "deep" and "figurative" for the average believer to understand? Do you believe Revelation 1 is only figurative or that it is intended as literal?

As the events known as 9-11 were unfolding, one Pastor and Preacher, David Jeremiah, as he observed the horror of people trapped and dying in two buildings that were becoming an inferno, gave the following responses: "That very day the lesson from Revelation chapter nine was, 'Hell on Earth.' When Satan is given permission to unlock the 'bottomless pit' of hell...the sky will be darkened by the hoard of demons. As the doors of hell are thrown open, the world is ravaged by these demonic terrorists. Looking through the smoky haze that surrounded the World Trade Center, I could almost superimpose the surreal picture of Revelation. I wondered - Could this terrorist attack be a wake-up call, reminding us that the prophecies of Revelation may not be as far out in the future as we think? You see, this was not an act of cowardice. It was not even terrorism. This was evil, a date with the devil. Perhaps this served as an emergency call for a nation that has been in a long sleep, a citizenry that for too long has been guilty of what the 19th century social activist (William Boetcker) called the Seven National Crimes: (1) I don't think; (2) I don't know; (3) I don't care; (4) I'm too busy; (5) I leave well enough alone; (6) I have no time to read and find out; (7) I'm not interested." Regrettably, these "Seven National Crimes" are all-too-common within our culture and the "church". The involvement with the things of God do not have the proper and adequate priority for ones life. There is a strange embrace of the malaise for the mediocre rather than a desire and longing for the absorption by that which is superior, without which one will continue is the drift and freefall away from the Lord and that which alone can and will satisfy.

The Psalmist had his finger on the pulse of the matter when he wrote – Psalm 42:1-5 – the soul searching words and the need for greater intimacy with the Lord. Note his words (Selected from The New Living Translation): "As the deer pants for streams of water, so I long for you, O God. I thirst for God, the living God. When can I come and stand before him? Day and night, I have only tears for food, while my enemies continually taunt me, saying, Where is this God of yours? My heart is breaking as I remember how it used to be: I walked among the crowds of worshipers, leading a great procession to the house of God, singing for joy and giving thanks -- it was the sound of a great celebration! Why am I discouraged? Why so sad? I will put my hope in God! I will praise him again -- my Savior and my God!"

An earlier chapter (Chapter 2) referenced "Thirsting For Je-sus" – the account of the Olford Family in Central Africa. The reality of thirst and the intense need for that thirst to be quenched by refreshing water. The application to the spiritual life and intimacy with Jesus is obvious, namely, "As the deer pants for streams of water, so my soul pants for you, O God. My soul thirsts for God, for the living God." This was one of the primary thrusts of Jesus when He instructed His followers in general, and His disciples in particular – Matthew 5:6 – "Blessed are those who hunger and thirst for righteousness, for they will be filled." The focus – "hunger and thirst for righ-teousness" – is basic and a necessity for each life – those who profess to follow Jesus Christ. The question for each one is in terms of the daily thirst for the Lord as the desire for intimacy continues to increase each day – Do you hunger and THIRST for the Lord?

The thoughts derived from this text are obvious: (a) What does your soul pant for? (b) What source do you seek out in order for your soul to be satisfied? (c) What do you believe will quench your thirst? (d) Is there a pre-set time when you can come to the Lord and seek to have your thirst quenched? (e) How often does your physical self need a refreshing drink of cool water? (f) Should your spiritual self require more or less than your physical self? (g) What is the best way to satisfy thirst – gulping or sipping?

The Psalmist cries out to the Lord – 143:1-6 (selected) – "Hear my prayer, O Lord; give ear to my pleas for mercy! In your faithfulness answer me, in your righteousness!...For the enemy has pursued my soul; he has crushed my life to the ground; he has made me sit in darkness like those long dead. Therefore my spirit faints within me; my heart within me is appalled. I remember the days of old; I meditate on all that you have done; I ponder the work of your hands. I stretch out my hands to you; my soul thirsts for you like a parched land..." Have you ever tried to work "parched land"? If you poured buckets of water on "parched land", would it tend to soak in or run off? What about spiritual thirst? Does it require one to be Taking A Serious God Seriously? Do you long for the steady and constant flow of water from Him so that your parched soul can absorb it and be benefitted by it? This becomes a result when one meditates in God's Word. Take note of Psalm 1:2-3 (NLT) where one gets the sense that the tap root goes deep and extends into the stream where there will be a constant supply of water. The Psalmist states: "But they (the godly/righteous) delight in doing everything the Lord wants; day and night they think about his law. They are like trees planted along the riverbank, bearing fruit each season without fail. Their leaves never wither, and in all they do, they prosper." Is this a description of you as you seek to quench your spiritual thirst from God and God Alone? Does this attest to the fact that you intend to be constant in Taking A Serious God Seriously?

The Lord has extended an invitation for each one to come to Him and He will freely respond, satisfy every longing and quench the greatest thirst. One of the several invitations is extended in Isaiah 55:1-3 (ESV), where the Lord says: "Come, everyone who thirsts, come to the waters; and he who has no money, come, buy and eat! Come, buy wine and milk without money and without price. Why do you spend your money for that which is not bread, and your labor for that which does not satisfy? Listen diligently to me, and eat what is good, and delight yourselves in rich food. Incline your ear, and come to me; hear, that your soul may live; and I will make with you an everlasting covenant, my steadfast, sure love for David." The

Message paraphrase renders this text as: "Hey there, all who are thirsty, come to the water! Are you penniless? Come anyway - buy and eat! Come, buy your drinks, buy wine and milk. Buy without money - everything's free! Why do you spend your money on junk food, your hard-earned cash on cotton candy? Listen to me, listen well: Eat only the best, fill yourself with only the finest. Pay attention, come close now, listen carefully to my life-giving, life-nourishing words. I'm making a lasting covenant commitment with you, the same that I made with David: sure, solid, enduring love." Isn't this something that you desire? Is an invitation to which you have responded? Is this one more opportunity where you can demonstrate that you will be Taking A Serious God Seriously?

When The Lord said in Isaiah 55, "I'm making a lasting co-venant commitment with you, the same that I made with David: sure, solid, enduring love." What is The Lord indicating and promising? The Davidic Covenant refers to God's promises to David through Nathan the prophet and is found in 2 Samuel 7:10-13. It is an unconditional covenant made between God and David through which God promises David and Israel that the Messiah (Jesus Christ) would come from the lineage of David and the tribe of Judah and would establish a kingdom that would endure forever. The Davidic Covenant is unconditional because God does not place any conditions of obedience upon its fulfillment. The surety of the promises made rests solely on God's faithfulness and does not depend at all on David or Israel's obedience. The provisions of the covenant are summarized in II Samuel 7:16 - "And your house and your kingdom shall be established forever before you. Your throne shall be established forever." The promise that David's house, kingdom and throne will be established forever is significant because it shows that the Messiah will come from the lineage of David and that He will establish a kingdom from which He will reign." The fulfillment of this Covenant made by the Lord with David is evidenced in the genealogy in Matthew 1:5-6 and 1:15-17 - "...and Salmon the father of Boaz by Rahab, and Boaz the father of Obed by Ruth, and Obed the father of Jesse, and Jesse the father of David the king. And David was the father of Solomon by the wife of Uriah... and Eliud the father of Eleazar, and Eleazar the father of Matthan, and Matthan the father of Jacob, and Jacob the father of Joseph the husband of Mary, of whom Jesus was born, who is called Christ. So all the generations from Abraham to David were fourteen generations, and from David to the deportation to Babylon fourteen generations, and from the deportation to Babylon to the Christ fourteen generations."

The genealogy is invaluable because one is able to see how the Lord chronicled carefully so that one can trace the Covenant from its inception up to its fulfillment. It is also evidence that God's Word is dependable. He doesn't make idle predictions and share wishful thinking. When God makes a Covenant, He is binding it on the basis of His Own Character because He cannot lie and will never misrepresent. The Davidic Covenant represents God's determination regarding the entry of the Only-Begotten-Son – Jesus Christ – into the world. The eternal purpose of the Son's entry was singular – that God might redeem a people for Himself. In I Peter 1:18-21 (ESV), "knowing that you were not redeemed with corruptible things, like silver or gold, from your aimless conduct received by tradition from your fathers, but with the precious blood of Christ, as of a lamb without blemish and without spot. He indeed was foreordained before the foundation of the world, but was manifest in these last times for you who through Him believe in God, who raised Him from the dead and gave Him glory, so that your faith and hope are in God." A key element regarding "when" this Covenant was determined is stated in verse 20, "He indeed was foreordained before the foundation of the world, but was manifest in these last times for you who through Him believe in God..." The NIV translates this verse: "He was chosen before the creation of the world, but was revealed in these last times for your sake." The New Living Translation is: "God chose him for this purpose long before the world began, but now in these final days, he was sent to the earth for all to see. And he did this for you..." The point is that a Covenant is not an afterthought but a revelation at a particular juncture with particular people that will find a future fulfillment to the Sovereign timing of God.

One should never approach the revelation of God with suspicion or subjectively. Revelation is always objective – God declaring what He wants us to know about Him and His purposes, and what He requires of each one of us who profess faith and trust in Him alone. We learn God's Revelation and Purpose from the Holy Scriptures alone. II Peter 1:19-21 declares, "And we have something more sure, the prophetic word, to which you will do well to pay attention as to a lamp shining in a dark place, until the day dawns and the morning star rises in your hearts, knowing this first of all, that no prophecy of Scripture comes from someone's own interpretation. For no prophecy was ever produced by the will of man, but men spoke from God as they were carried along by the Holy Spirit." The Holy Scriptures are our Manual for Life. If we fail to consult the Manual, we will know what malfunction is all about. Near to where I reside, there are different Highways and Interstates that intersect in one place. The intent of the design and the ensuing result has allowed the "locals" to refer to this convergence as being The Malfunction Junction. It is an appropriate name – especially when rush hour traffic attempts to navigate through it. With the best GPS (Global Positioning System) devices, one still cannot gain an advantage in passing through The Malfunction Junction.

The application for one's life is obvious. Too often, when one has neglected to refer to the Holy Scriptures, there are The Malfunction Junction moments and experiences. Earlier in this Chapter, reference was made to the "Seven National Crimes: (1) I don't think; (2) I don't know; (3) I don't care; (4) I'm too busy; (5) I leave well enough alone; (6) I have no time to read and find out; (7) I'm not interested." These all represent apathy, indifference and malfunction. If one is Taking A Serious God Seriously, there should be – will be – the desire to seek remedy and make correction for the betterment of one's life. There will be the sincere effort to take the negative attitudes and characteristics and endeavor to have them become positives. It will mean the "Seven National Crimes" will be converted to "Seven Positive Traits and Attitudes" for meaningful life and practical function. A starting point will be: (1) to implement Philippians 4:8 and begin to think on the virtuous things – "...if anything is excellent or praiseworthy--think about such things." (2) to realize the meaning of Proverbs 1:7, "The fear of the LORD is the beginning of knowledge..." (3) to demonstrate meaningful care for others as one puts into practice Galatians 6:2 and begins to " Carry each other's burdens, and in this way you will fulfill the law of Christ." (4) There will be revamped priorities for one's life and greater discipline with time management. There will be a keen awareness in regard to the value in grasping Ecclesiastes 3:1-8, " There is a time for everything, and a season for every activity under heaven..." (5) The moments in time when one should be involved and engaged. The idea of this is given in James 2:14-26, "...Suppose a brother or sister is without clothes and daily food. If one of you says to him, Go, I wish you well; keep warm and well fed, but does nothing about his physical needs, what good is it? In the same way, faith by itself, if it is not accompanied by action, is dead..." (6) There must be time scheduled when one reads the Manual – The Holy Scriptures.

A challenge is given in II Timothy 2:13-16, "... Be diligent (study) to present yourself approved to God, a worker who does not need to be ashamed, rightly dividing the word of truth..." It's following the example of the Berean believers in Acts 17:10-12, "These were more fair-minded than those in Thessalonica, in that they received the word with all readiness, and searched the Scriptures daily to find out whether these things were so." (7) One must have an interest in the things that must be a priority for life. It involves a commitment as one Follows Jesus Christ and is made a disciple by Him. Luke 14:26-35 sets the parameters of both following and being a disciple. It entails making a choice and a commitment to Jesus Christ alone. It will define the one who is Taking A Serious God Seriously.

QUESTIONS FOR THOUGHT AND APPLICATION

1. The concern of this Book has been whether or not the church, congregant, community or culture is Taking A Serious God Seriously. Previous chapters have focused on light and what it is supposed to do. If a light bulb is removed from a lamp, will going through the motion of turning the switch on the lamp make any difference? Why?

2. If or when darkness is tolerated and preferred, it is indicative of a lifestyle choice and desire. Generally, why would a person prefer darkness to light? Would it imply there is something about which they are ashamed? Would it suggest there is some anticipated deed that they would hope would not be observed?

3. In John 3:18-21, there is a distinction drawn between Light and Darkness. It is couched in terms of "this is the condemnation..."

(a)   What has come into the world?
(b)   What have men preferred?
(c)   Why is this their choice and preference?

4. For those for whom there is commendation – Vs. 21 – could we insert the phrase – "this is the commendation..."

(a)   What is the commended one doing?
(b)   What about his/her deeds – is there anything that needs to be hidden?
(c)   In Whom has this one's deeds been done?

5. Citing Examples of Malfunction among the People of God:

(a)   Exodus 32 – what was the thinking of the people that resulted in their malfunction and the golden calf becoming their choice and focus?

(b)   I Kings 18 – what was the thinking of the people whose malfunction was uttering not a word in regard to the prophets of Baal and worship of a foreign god?

(c)   In Galatians 1 through 3 – what was the influence of the "legalists" that allowed for the malfunction among those whom Paul rebuked – "having begun in the Spirit, are you now made perfect in the flesh"?

6.   The Book of Malachi closes with these words (3:18), "Then you shall again discern between the righteous and the wicked, between one who serves God And one who does not serve Him." As the ministry of Jesus begins, He gives a Sermon on the Mount – Matthew 5 through 7. In Matthew 5:6 is one of the Beatitudes that echoes some of the words of Malachi, namely: "Blessed are those who hunger and thirst for righteousness, for they shall be filled." What is involved and entailed for the one who is hungering and thirsting for righteousness?

What does Malachi indicate the righteous will do?

What does Jesus say the righteous will gain?

Is "hungering and thirsting" a theory or a disciplined act?

How long will it take to accomplish the desired goal of righteousness in and for one's life?

7.   In Psalm 42:1-5, what does the Psalmist liken the process of seeking after and desiring of righteousness? Is it a desire or a pursuit? What is the status of the "deer" in Psalm 42?

There is therefore now no condemnation to those who are in Christ Jesus, who do not walk according to the flesh, but according to the Spirit.

Romans 8:1

But God demonstrates (commends) His own love toward us, in that while we were still sinners, Christ died for us.

Romans 5:8

Redemptive Plan

The words stated in Hebrews 6:17-20 are both helpful and encouraging: "...when God desired to show more convincingly to the heirs of the promise the unchangeable character of his purpose, he guaranteed it with an oath, so that by two unchangeable things, in which it is impossible for God to lie, we who have fled for refuge might have strong encouragement to hold fast to the hope set before us. We have this as a sure and steadfast anchor of the soul, a hope that enters into the inner place behind the curtain, where Jesus has gone as a forerunner on our behalf..."

In terms of being "heirs of the promise" and to make the connection between the Covenant made with Abraham and the application of that Covenant with us today, note the words of Galatians 3:25-29 – "But now that faith has come, we are no longer under a guardian, for in Christ Jesus you are all sons of God, through faith. For as many of you as were baptized into Christ have put on Christ. There is neither Jew nor Greek, there is neither slave nor free, there is no male and female, for you are all one in Christ Jesus. And if you are Christ's, then you are Abraham's offspring, heirs according to promise."

What are the foundational truths regarding Redemption. We read in I John 2:2 and 4:10 (ESV): "He is the propitiation for our sins, and not for ours only but also for the sins of the whole world." – and – "In this is love, not that we have loved God but that he loved us and sent his Son to be the propitiation for our sins." If Jesus is our "propitiation", what exactly is He and what does that mean? The (NIV) gives a different statement for "propitiation" by stating the Son is the "...atoning sacrifice for our sins..."

The technical definition of the terms is: "Christ is called the 'propitiation for our sins.' The Greek word used here is (hilasmos). Christ is "the propitiation," because by his becoming our substitute and assuming our obligations he expiated our guilt, covered it, by the vicarious punishment which he endured and satisfied God's requirement and demand for divine justice..." With Expiation, the technical meaning is: " Guilt is said to be expiated when it is visited with punishment falling on a substitute. Expiation is made for our sins when they are punished not in ourselves but in another who consents to stand in our room. It is that by which reconciliation is effected. Sin is thus said to be "covered" by vicarious satisfaction..." Guilt is removed by the substitutionary death of Christ who made the payment for our personal sin when He gave Himself in His death on the Cross – the debt was paid and God was satisfied. The idea is found in what Paul wrote – II Corinthians 5:21 – "God made him who had no sin to be sin for us, so that in him we might become the righteousness of God (in Him)."

As God's Redemptive Plan is being revealed to us, the great truths we learn are several. Among them are: Ephesians 1:6-8 (NKJV), "...to the praise of the glory of His grace, by which He made us accepted in the Beloved. In Him we have redemption through His blood, the forgiveness of sins, according to the riches of His grace which He made to abound toward us..." It is an absolute statement, namely, Jesus Christ was made to be our redemption and He is all that we need. We also note this truth in Colossians 1:5-6, "the hope which is laid up for you in heaven, of which you heard before in the word of the truth of the gospel, which has come to you, as it has also in all the world, and is bringing forth fruit, as it is also among you since the day you heard and knew the grace of God in truth…" The truth of the Gospel has brought forth fruit through our lives and given us hope of everlasting life. One additional passage of God's Word that underscores the means and cost of this redemption in Jesus Christ is in II Corinthians 5:14-18, "For the love of Christ compels us, because we judge thus: that if One died for all, then all died; and He died for all, that those who live should live no longer for themselves, but for Him who died for them and rose again. Therefore, from now on, we regard no one according to the flesh. Even though we have known Christ according to the flesh, yet now we know Him thus no longer. Therefore, if anyone is in Christ, he is a new creation; old things have passed away; behold, all things have become new. Now all things are of God, who has reconciled us to Himself through Jesus Christ,.."

II Corinthians 5:15 has to be one of the most succinct and plain statements of one's redemption and the implication of that redemption as one implements the great truth of the Gospel – "…He died for all, that those who live should live no longer for themselves, but for Him who died for them and rose again." The New Living Translation is, "He died for everyone so that those who receive his new life will no longer live to please themselves. Instead, they will live to please Christ, who died and was raised for them."

In 1977, Archie P. Jordan wrote the lyric to a song that was first sung by Amy Grant and became popular within the Christian Music genre. Later on, Ronnie Milsap presented it in the country Gospel genre where it gained even greater popularity. It has a veiled reference to the difference the redemptive work of Jesus Christ will make in one's life. The point and thrust is

that man stands at a crossroad in his life where a choice must
be made – to either life for oneself or to live for Jesus Christ.
Some of the Lyric is - - -

> What a difference you've made in my life
> What a difference you've made in my life
> You're my sunshine day and night
> Oh what a difference you've made in my life.

> What a change you have made in my heart
> What a change you have made in my heart
> You replaced all the broken parts
> Oh what a change you have made in my heart.

> Love to me was just a word in a song
> That had been way over-used
> But now I've joined in the singin'
> 'Cause you've shown me love's true meanin'
> That's why I want to spread the news

> What a difference you've made in my life
> What a difference you've made in my life
> You're my sunshine day and night
> Oh what a difference you've made in my life.

When one thinks of the foundational truths of faith, the activity of the contemporary world and culture should not be
allowed to influence the principles of faith or cause one to shift
or to doubt. A question worthy of consideration is, How Firm
Are The Foundations Of Your Life? Another question is, How
Firmly Situated Are You In Terms Of Eternity? In March 2011,
the unthinkable and unimaginable occurred without warning.
Suddenly, Japan experienced a 9.0 earthquake, followed by a

Tsunami Wave that reached up to 30 feet destroying every-thing in its path. Between the earthquake and tsunami, four nuclear power plants were impacted and radiation began to infiltrate the atmosphere. The coastline of Japan shifted and the earth moved on its axis. Thousands of people were killed and are missing. It all happened quickly, suddenly, unexpected-ly, with no time for preparation.

Then in September 2011, an unexpected earthquake oc-curred leaving people shaken from the Carolinas up into Canada. There was hardly enough time to begin to recover from the earthquakes when the Hurricane Katia struck the East Coast and brought flood waters that had not been seen for many years. People were shaken and many suffered the loss of their treasured possessions. It is vital and of great importance that one's spiritual foundations remain firm and regardless of the impact of nature's force upon the temporal – we have an anchor that keeps us safe and secure. In Hebrews 12:25-28, there are significant words shared with us – "See that you do not refuse him who is speaking. For if they did not escape when they refused him who warned them on earth, much less will we escape if we reject him who warns from heaven. At that time his voice shook the earth, but now he has promised, Yet once more I will shake not only the earth but also the heavens. This phrase, Yet once more, indicates the removal of things that are shaken--that is, things that have been made--in order that the things that cannot be shaken may remain. Therefore let us be grateful for receiving a kingdom that cannot be shaken, and thus let us offer to God acceptable worship, with reverence and awe,.." The words are clear and precisely spoken: "At that time his voice shook the earth, but now he has promised, Yet once more I will shake not only the earth but also the heavens."

In the grand consideration of Redemption In Christ Jesus, there should be something of substance that serves as the foundation for ones life. The words stated in Hebrews 6:17-20 are both helpful and encouraging: "…when God desired to show more convincingly to the heirs of the promise the unchangeable character of his purpose, he guaranteed it with an oath, so that by two unchangeable things, in which it is impossible for God to lie, we who have fled for refuge might have strong encouragement to hold fast to the hope set before us. We have this as a sure and steadfast anchor of the soul, a hope that enters into the inner place behind the curtain, where Jesus has gone as a forerunner on our behalf…" How Great and Firm is this Foundation! Previous reference was made to the Hymn: How Firm A Foundation? It merits notice once again because one so easily forgets that foundation and attempts to cope with and live life horizontally - on the threshold of quick sand – rather than vertically – on the Solid Rock. Note once again two stanzas from the Hymn – How Firm A Foundation - and be encouraged and blest as you remind yourself of God's Power and Promise for all who believe - - -

"Fear not, I am with thee, O be not dismayed;
I, I am thy God, and will still give thee aid;
I'll strengthen thee, help thee, and cause thee to stand,
Upheld by my righteous, omnipotent hand.

"The soul that on Jesus hath leaned for repose,
I will not, I will not desert to his foes;
That soul, though all hell should endeavor to shake,
I'll never, no, never, no, never forsake."

There is only one way to arrive at a determination that demonstrates both the reality and benefit of the firm foundation, namely, (1) counting the cost, (2) making the right choice and (3) being fully committed to The One Who made the firm foundation viable. The Lord Jesus Christ spoke of the firm foundation as He instructed His disciples in terms of their lifetime commitment to and for Him. In Matthew 7:24-27, Jesus taught: "Everyone then who hears these words of mine and does them will be like a wise man who built his house on the rock. And the rain fell, and the floods came, and the winds blew and beat on that house, but it did not fall, because it had been founded on the rock. And everyone who hears these words of mine and does not do them will be like a foolish man who built his house on the sand. And the rain fell, and the floods came, and the winds blew and beat against that house, and it fell, and great was the fall of it."

It is obvious from this instruction that one has only two choices for a foundation – either rock or sand. In very simple terms, the lesson Jesus is sharing is basic regarding any building project. The architect will establish what can be done; the engineer will calculate where it should be done; and the draftsman will draw a concept of what it will look like after it is done. The failure to exercise care regarding the choice of location and place for the foundation can have a drastic and catastrophic consequence. One example is The Leaning Tower of Pisa in Italy. The assessment was that "...due to errors in design, construction, or to subsequent external influence – the Tower does not stand perpendicular to the ground...The Tower began to sink after construction had progressed to the second floor...This was due to a mere three-meter foundation, set in weak, unstable sub-soil – a design that was flawed from the beginning..."

Jesus instructed that one must choose the foundation for one's lifetime commitment carefully and wisely. The choices seem so obvious – rock or sand - that it's difficult to imagine why one would choose anything other than the obvious, namely, the foundation of solid rock. Jesus is abundantly clear in what He is stating. It begins with "...hears these words of Mine..." In a way, this lesson foreshadows what will be a recurring phrase in Revelation 2 and 3 – "He who has an ear, let him hear what the Spirit says to the churches. To the one who conquers I will grant to eat of the tree of life, which is in the paradise of God."

One other consideration in the instruction by Jesus pertains to the result of the construction site and choice. If the choice has been the rock, what has been built will be able to withstand the strong winds and deluge of rain. Jesus said – "that house...did not fall." However, the one who did not exercise care and wisdom in the choice of the site will one day regret his lack of care in planning and building. Why? Because when the strong winds blow and the heavy rains fall and beat against that structure, Jesus said – "that house...fell, and great was the fall of it."

The choices one makes are vital both for this life and eternity. There is an old saying: "The proof of the pudding is in the tasting." In regard to the "Christian" life, the proof of one's "Christianity" is in terms of what is observable. In one of his Devotional Writings, Dr. A. W. Tozer (1897-1963) wrote about the distinctiveness of the Christian life and commitment to Jesus Christ as compared to that which is too often observed. He wrote: "Millions call themselves by His name, it is true, and pay some token respect to Him, but a simple test will show how little He is really honored among them. Let the average man be put to the proof on the question of who or what is above, and his true position will be exposed. Let him be forced into making a choice between God and money, God and men, between God and personal ambition, God and self, God and human love, and God will take second place every time. Those other things will be exalted above. However the man may protest, the proof is in the choices he makes day after day throughout his life." This is the bottom-line issue for each of us – our choices and priorities – what has first-place in one's life?

The issue of life choices is very important. Too often, the subjective – what I want – dominates the objective – that which is right and best for me. There are places in God's Word where choices are mentioned as well as the process and tension by which and through which a decision is reached. First, Paul shares the ongoing struggle in the Christian life regarding right and wrong, commitment and compromise. Romans 7:15-25 describes Paul's struggle: " For I do not understand my own actions. For I do not do what I want, but I do the very thing I hate. Now if I do what I do not want, I agree with the law, that it is good. So now it is no longer I who do it, but sin that dwells within me. For I know that nothing good dwells in me, that is, in my flesh. For I have the desire to do what is right, but not the ability to carry it out. For I do not do the good I want, but the evil I do not want is what I keep on doing. Now if I do what I do not want, it is no longer I who do it, but sin that dwells within me. So I find it to be a law that when I want to do right, evil lies close at hand. For I delight in the law of God, in my inner being, but I see in my members another law waging war against the law of my mind and making me captive to the law of sin that dwells in my members. Wretched man that I am! Who will deliver me from this body of death? Thanks be to God through Jesus Christ our Lord! So then, I myself serve the law of God with my mind, but with my flesh I serve the law of sin." Most can identify with Paul and the struggles between doing the will of God and coping with the deeds of the flesh. We need to be on the firm foundation of verse 24-25, "Who will deliver me from this body of death? Thanks be to God through Jesus Christ our Lord!"

This matter of choices arises in Paul's life as he ponders Heaven and the joy of being in the presence of the Lord versus continuing with fruitful ministry on earth. This struggle and tension is shared in Philippians 1:22-25, "If I am to live in the flesh, that means fruitful labor for me. Yet which I shall choose I cannot tell. I am hard pressed between the two. My desire is to depart and be with Christ, for that is far better. But to remain in the flesh is more necessary on your account. Convinced of this, I know that I will remain and continue with you all, for your progress and joy in the faith." The last phrase in this passage is very meaningful – "your progress and joy in the faith." To arrive at the point where it is God's will and not my will, and the complete abandonment to verse 20, "...it is my eager expectation and hope that I will not be at all ashamed, but that with full courage now as always Christ will be honored in my body, whether by life or by death." Christ Honored - - Christ Magnified in my body - - by life or by death. This is the firm foundation! This is the correct choice! This is arriving at the place where your progress and joy in the faith is complete and satisfied.

There is an extended passage regarding right choices and firm foundations in Joshua 24:14-27. Joshua is challenging the children of God to avoid the negative influences in the land and to follow the Lord and His Word as the sole influence in and for one's life. Joshua declares to the people: "Now therefore fear the Lord and serve him in sincerity and in faithfulness. Put away the gods that your fathers served beyond the River and in Egypt, and serve the Lord. And if it is evil in your eyes to serve the Lord, choose this day whom you will serve, whether the gods your fathers served in the region beyond the River, or the gods of the Amorites in whose land you dwell. But as for me and my house, we will serve the Lord." Joshua has stated the choice so clearly that the answer can and should be immediate and emphatic. None of those being challenge can claim they have forgotten all of what the Lord has done for them since they left Egypt to this place of a threshold choice. The Message paraphrases verse 15, "If you decide that it's a bad thing to worship God, then choose a god you'd rather serve - and do it today. Choose one of the gods your ancestors worshiped from the country beyond The River, or one of the gods of the Amorites, on whose land you're now living. As for me and my family, we'll worship God." In effect, Joshua is saying, let The River serve as your Rubicon (The idiom — Crossing The Rubicon — means to pass a point of no return and no retreat. The reference is to Julius Caesar's army crossing the River in 49 BC. Attempting to return or retreat was considered an Act of Insurrection).

The people respond to Joshua — verses 16-18 — "Then the people answered, Far be it from us that we should forsake the Lord to serve other gods, for it is the Lord our God who brought us and our fathers up from the land of Egypt, out of the house of slavery, and who did those great signs in our sight and preserved us in all the way that we went, and among all the peoples through whom we passed. And the Lord drove out before us all the peoples, the Amorites who lived in the land. Therefore we also will serve the Lord, for he is our God." The people rehearse their history and traditions. They are giving

the correct answer to the challenge placed before them. But –
will they follow through and/or for how long will this response
be their foundation of their faith?

Joshua becomes even more emphatic. He wants the people
to clearly understand that they are responding to The Eternal
God and His requirements for worship and service are extensive and comprehensive. In verses 19-27 (selected), Joshua
defines what they are establishing and with Whom it is being
established: "Joshua said to the people, You are not able to
serve the Lord, for he is a Holy God. He is a jealous God; he will
not forgive your transgressions or your sins. If you forsake the
Lord and serve foreign gods, then He will turn and do you harm
and consume you, after having done you good. And the people
said to Joshua, No, but we will serve the Lord. Then Joshua said
to the people, You are witnesses against yourselves that you
have chosen the Lord, to serve him. And they said, We are
witnesses..." This is their profession – but – what about their
practice? It's no longer just what they say but also what they
will continually do! In verses 23-27, Joshua continues, "...Then
put away the foreign gods that are among you, and incline your
heart to the Lord, the God of Israel. And the people said to
Joshua, The Lord our God we will serve, and his voice we will
obey... Joshua made a covenant with the people that day, and
put in place statutes and rules for them..."

This is their defining moment! This is their opportunity of
foundation selection! This is the time to look at The River as
their Rubicon – the place of no turning back and no retreat!
This is their choice and decision is to serve the Lord and no
longer compromise the foundations of their faith! Have you
come to such a moment in your life? Have you crossed your
Rubicon of no turning back and no retreat? Your choice and

your decision can be made now to serve the Lord and to no longer compromise the foundations of your faith.

QUESTIONS FOR THOUGHT AND APPLICATION

1. In I Peter 1:17-21, there is a synopsis of God's Redemptive Plan.

- What was the acceptable sacrifice for our Redemption (Vs. 19)?
- When was this Plan and Provision established (Vs. 20)?
- When was it Manifested? For whom was it Manifested (Vs. 20)?
- Would this sacrifice have been beneficial if it had remained dead (Vs. 21)?
- What was this sacrifice given when He was raised from the dead (Vs. 21)?
- What does that mean for one's relationship to and with God (Vs. 21)?

2. There are two theological terms used in terms of one's redemption – Propitiation (God's Divine justice is satisfied) and Expiation (Christ's work in removing man's Guilt for sin by the payment of a penalty).

The Holman Bible Dictionary states: "...the doctrine of the atonement includes both the dimensions of propitiation - averting the wrath of God - and expiation - taking away or covering over human guilt. By the expiation of human guilt, the wrath of God is turned away, the holiness of God is satisfied. Yet it is God who in the person of His Son performs the sacrifice of expiation. It is God who in the person of His Son swallows up evil within Himself through vicarious identification with the sin of His people. A sacrifice was necessary to satisfy the demands of His law, but God Himself provided the Sacrifice out of His incomparable love."

SEE: Isaiah 53:10-11

Vs. 10: What two things did it please the Lord to do to The Suffering Servant?

Vs. 11 (a): What will God see/be because of the Sacrifice of Jesus Christ?

Vs. 11(b): What will the righteous servant do/accomplish?

Vs. 11(c) : What will the righteous servant bear?

3.   Ephesians 1:6-8 contains a summary of what is available in and through Jesus Christ. What three truths do you glean from Vs. 7? We have - - -
(a)
(b)
(c)

4.   If Redemption is a reality in one's life, it should include particular and defining moments for the individual.

(a)   Colossians 3:1-4 - How is your life in Christ described? What is your redeemed mindset supposed to be?

(b)   Colossians 3:5-9 - What is the Redeemed person required to put off?

(c)   Colossians 3:10 - What is the Redeemed person required to put on?

(d)   Colossians 3:12-17 - What are the new qualities and characteristics (you could find as many as 12 in these verses) of the Redeemed person?

5.   Which set of qualities and characteristics best defines you?

His divine power has given us everything we need for life and godliness through our knowledge of him who called us by his own glory and goodness. Through these he has given us his very great and precious promises, so that through them you may participate in the divine nature and escape the corruption in the world caused by evil desires. For this very reason, make every effort to add to your faith goodness...knowledge;...self-control... perseverance...godliness...brotherly kindness...love...If you possess these qualities in increasing measure, they will keep you from being ineffective and unproductive in your knowledge of our Lord Jesus Christ. But if anyone does not have them, he is nearsighted and blind, and has forgotten that he has been cleansed from his past sins. Therefore...be all the more eager to make your calling and election sure. For if you do these things, you will never fall...

II Peter 1:3-10

Transition and Adaptation

I call to remembrance my song in the night; I meditate within my heart, And my spirit makes diligent search. Will the Lord cast off forever? And will He be favorable no more? Has His mercy ceased forever? Has His promise failed forevermore? Has God forgotten to be gracious? Has He in anger shut up His tender mercies?
Psalm 77:6-9

Restore us, O God of our salvation, And cause Your anger toward us to cease. Will You be angry with us forever? Will You prolong Your anger to all generations? Will You not revive us again, That Your people may rejoice in You? Show us Your mercy, Lord, And grant us Your salvation. I will hear what God the Lord will speak, For He will speak peace To His people and to His saints; But let them not turn back to folly.
Psalm 85:4-8

If one is to proceed and advance with Taking A Serious God Seriously, it will entail the embrace of several truths – the standards and requirements of the Lord for His People. When Jesus Christ is walking in the midst of the seven churches – Revelation 1 through 3 – as He considers the actions and behavior of His people, and as He makes His assessment, He summarizes by stating (Revelation 2:5) – " Remember therefore from where you have fallen; repent and do the first works, or else I will come to you quickly and remove your lamp-stand from its place--unless you repent." Quite simply, the call is to (a) Remember, (b) Repent, and (c) Return. It is addressing the relationship one has with Christ and the commitment one has made to submit to Him in all things so that He will have the preeminence in one's life. It will require self-examination and the squaring of one's life with the Word of God. J.B. Phillips renders it – "Remember then how far you have fallen. Repent and live as you lived at first. Otherwise, if your heart remains unchanged, I shall come to you and remove your lamp-stand from its place.

A place where self-examination can begin is in Prayer and Inquiry. In Psalm 77, the Psalmist ponders his life and relationship to the Lord with intimate and particular questions - - -
- Will the Lord cast us off forever?
- Will He be favorable no more?
- Has His mercy ceased forever?
- Has the promise failed forevermore?
- Has God forgotten to be gracious?
- Has He in anger shut up His tender mercies?

The Psalmist continues with his self-examination and pondering additional questions in Psalm 85 - - -
- Will You be angry with us forever?
- Will You prolong Your anger to all generations?
- Will you not revive us again, that Your people may rejoice in You?

He longs to have his heart and life right with the Lord. He wants to walk in step with the Lord and to continually walk in the light as He is in the light. This process of self-examination is similar to the heart-cry of the Psalmist in Psalm 139:23-24, "Search me, O God, and know my heart! Try me and know my thoughts! And see if there be any grievous way in me, and lead me in the way everlasting!"

Is this your heart-cry? Are these the things that you seek for in your relationship and walk with the Lord Jesus Christ? When you pray and meditate, do you ponder your life and relationship with the Lord, and inquire in terms of intimate and particular questions regarding your faith and practice? As one ponders all of these things before God – and as you practice Taking The Serious God Seriously – one will become more keenly aware of God's Word, God's Will and God's Plan for one's life!

One of the major concerns discussed in an earlier chapter in this tome concerns the use of the right terms apart from the reality of the right actions and walk in one's life. When this begins to occur, there tends to be a drifting away from the foundational truths and moorings. In Hebrews 2:1-4, an alert and warning is given regarding departure from the foundational truths: "…we must pay much closer attention to what we have heard, lest we drift away from it. For since the message declared by angels proved to be reliable, and every transgression or disobedience received a just retribution, how shall we escape if we neglect such a great salvation? It was declared at first by the Lord, and it was attested to us by those who heard, while God also bore witness by signs and wonders and various miracles and by gifts of the Holy Spirit distributed according to his will."

There is an interesting historical reference that gives a hint and statement on what will occur if a democracy begins to blur its focus and compromise its values. The quotation has a question attached to it because of attribution (who actually made the statement, etc.) . As best as it can be determined, two sources have the following compiled idea regarding the drift and cycle of nations and democracies: "Two centuries ago, a somewhat obscure Scotsman named Alexander Fraser Tytler made this profound observation: A democracy cannot exist as a permanent form of government. It can only exist until the majority discovers it can vote itself largess out of the public treasury. After that, the majority always votes for the candidate promising the most benefits with the result the democracy collapses because of the loose fiscal policy ensuing, always to be followed by a dictatorship, then a monarchy." The section of the statement often attributed to Tytler became known as the "Tytler Cycle" or the "Fatal Sequence". However, "...Its first known appearance is in a 1943 speech "Industrial Management in a Republic" by H. W. Prentis, president of the Armstrong Cork Company and former president of the National Association of Manufacturers," It is alleged that the "Cycle" or "Sequence" was formulated by him and indicates: "The average age of the world's greatest civilizations from the beginning of history, has been about 200 years. During those 200 years, these nations always progressed through the following sequence: From bondage to spiritual faith; From spiritual faith to great courage; From courage to liberty; From liberty to abundance; From abundance to complacency; From complacency to apathy; From apathy to dependence; From dependence back into bondage." Regardless of who formulated the "cycle" or "sequence", the formulation has historical validity. It seems to be especially true when nations begin to forget God and either squeeze Him out of the public discourse or remove Him altogether. In such instances, God become irrelevant to the culture, and sadly, that cultural mindset infiltrates the "Christian community" that is continued to be known as the "church". This begins to occur when the nation and church drifts away from Taking A Serious God Seriously.

For both the nation and the "church", what must be remembered? What is basic for both? What must be determined and done? There is a clear choice set before God's people in Deuteronomy 11:1-3, 26-28. It speaks of the clear choice and alternative results. "You shall therefore love the Lord your God and keep His charge, His statutes, His rules, and His command-ments always. And consider today (since I am not speaking to your children who have not known or seen it), consider the discipline of the Lord your God, His greatness, His mighty hand and His outstretched arm, His signs and His deeds that He did in Egypt to Pharaoh...and to all his land...Behold, I set before you today a blessing and a curse - the blessing, if you obey the commandments of the Lord your God which I command you today; and the curse, if you do not obey the commandments of the Lord your God, but turn aside from the way which I com-mand you today, to go after other gods which you have not known."

One of the Issues of our day – Wrong Choices. In the intro-duction of this book - Taking A Serious God Seriously – I wrote the following: "It is incumbent upon every generation to be attuned to the voice of God – to know Him and to discern His will. When we do so, one should then effectively be equipped to make Him known. If one cannot, the question is: "Why not?" The timidity and reluctance of those who call themselves "the people of God" has contributed unwittingly to the ineffective-ness of the "church" and the collapse of the culture and the demise of moral values."

In Psalm 99 – the Psalmist remembers: "Moses and Aaron were among His priests, Samuel also was among those who called upon His name. They called to the Lord, and He ans-wered them. In the pillar of the cloud He spoke to them; they kept His testimonies and the statute that He gave them. O Lord our God, You answered them; You were a forgiving God to them, but an avenger of their wrongdoings. Exalt the Lord our God, and worship at His holy mountain; for the Lord our God is holy!" A key point being made is: God Answered and Spoke To Them. Do you hear His voice? Do you see the evidences of His handiwork? Are you looking? Are you listening? Are You Taking A Serious God Seriously? Are you making a forthright and unambiguous commitment – to be serious with a serious God?

There's an important and serious discussion in terms of "the people of God" and how a generation of them grew complacent – matter-of-fact – with God and His Word. Ezra and Nehemiah have been given the task to rebuild both a wall and a nation of people. In Nehemiah 9:16-17, how the nation (and "church") got where it is – as it failed to be faithful and functional according to God's terms and requirements. Note: "...our forefathers, became arrogant and stiff-necked, and did not obey your commands. They refused to listen and failed to remember the miracles you performed among them. They became stiff-necked and in their rebellion appointed a leader in order to return to their slavery." The Failure was their refusal and Inability to listen, discern, comprehend and apply God's Truth for their lives. They failed to remember and they began to drift – driven by the tide and sentiment of that day.

I Timothy 4:1-2, we are given the sense of both that day and ours. Paul writes: "The Spirit clearly says that in later times some will abandon the faith and follow deceiving spirits and things taught by demons. Such teachings come through hypocritical liars, whose consciences have been seared as with a hot iron." The Message rendering is: "The Spirit makes it clear that as time goes on, some are going to give up on the faith and chase after demonic illusions put forth by professional liars. These liars have lied so well and for so long that they've lost their capacity for truth." The Revival Preacher – Charles Finney (1900s) – Indicated in his treatise on The Seared Conscience: "A man may know his duty, without feeling impelled by an emphatic affirmation of moral obligation to do it. He may know that he is or has been wrong, without the consciousness of being arraigned, convicted of guilt, and condemned. This state of mind clearly indicates a seared conscience."

To what can one appeal? What is a constant in terms of God? In Nehemiah 9:17b-20, he brings to remembrance the compassion of The Faithful God. We note: "But you are a forgiving God, gracious and compassionate, slow to anger and abounding in love. Therefore You did not desert them, even when they cast for themselves an image of a calf and said, 'This is your god, who brought you up out of Egypt,' or when they committed awful blasphemies. "Because of Your Great Compassion You did not abandon them in the desert. By day the pillar of cloud did not cease to guide them on their path, nor the pillar of fire by night to shine on the way they were to take...You gave your good Spirit to instruct them; You did not withhold your manna from their mouths, and You gave them water for their thirst."

The nation, culture and "church" should gratefully remember – The Nature and Character of God. This truth is established and emphasized I II Timothy 2:11-13, "The saying is trustworthy, for: If we have died with him, we will also live with him; if we endure, we will also reign with him; if we deny him, he also will deny us; if we are faithless, he remains faithful--for he cannot deny himself." The key thought is: God remains faithful – He CANNOT deny Himself. Once this truth is believed and implemented within the culture and/or "church", it would be appropriate for a twofold Confession to follow: (a) Confession and Acknowledgement of one's sins, and (b) Confession of Faith as one enters into a purposeful relationship with The God Who CANNOT deny Himself. An example of an acceptable Confession and Reflection in behalf of the people begins in Nehemiah 9: 30-33 – "For many years You were patient with them. By Your Spirit You admonished them through Your prophets. Yet they paid no attention, so You handed them over to the neighboring peoples. But in Your great mercy you did not put an end to them or abandon them, for You are a gracious and merciful God. Now therefore, O our God, the great, mighty and awesome God, Who keeps his covenant of love, do not let all this hardship seem trifling in Your eyes–the hardship that has come upon us, upon our kings and leaders, upon our priests and prophets, upon our fathers and all Your people, from the days of the kings of Assyria until today. In all that has happened to us, You have been just; you have acted faithfully, while we did wrong."

The Question emerges: What Did The People Need To DO To Get Back On Track? We begin to get a hint of what they needed to do in Nehemiah 8:2-3. When People begin to Respond, To Remember, Repent and To Return: "...on the first day of the seventh month Ezra the priest brought the Law before the assembly, which was made up of men and women and all who were able to understand. He read it aloud from daybreak till noon as he faced the square before the Water Gate in the presence of the men, women and others who could understand..." The key for any time of Remembrance, Repentance and Returning is: "...all the people listened attentively to the Book of the Law..." It meant getting one's Life aligned with The Word Of God. It would mean that life could no longer lived "My Way" - but from this point forward - it is God's Way from now on – and – forever. The theme of one's life becomes: Not I, But

Christ. The words from a Hymn written in 1891 reminds one of this lifetime commitment to The Lord - - -

Not I, but Christ, be honored, loved, exalted;
Not I, but Christ, be seen be known, be heard;
Not I, but Christ, in every look and action,
Not I, but Christ, in every thought and word.

The Refrain - - -
O to be saved from myself, dear Lord,
O to be lost in Thee,
O that it might be no more I,
But Christ, that lives in me.

As the Word of God was read, the people wept. Their drifting away from God had been considerable - so great had been their neglect and rebellion. They had permitted themselves to miss so much of what is vital for one's life, namely, the Lord and His Word. They wept because of what they had so carelessly ignored and avoided. They wept as they became more aware of both God's compassion and His forgiveness of their sin. They were experiencing first-hand the full measure of His love, His mercy and His grace. They were at a place where they could begin again and could implement all of what it means to be Taking A Serious God Seriously.

The best message and preaching in the world must have the guidance of the Holy Spirit and His using it to make God's application in the lives of those hearing it. The lurking question is: What will the people do and how will they respond to The Word from the Lord. In Nehemiah 8:8-12, "Ezra read from the Book of the Law of God, making it clear and giving the meaning so that the people could understand what was being read.

Then Nehemiah the governor, Ezra the priest and scribe, and the Levites who were instructing the people said to them all: This day is sacred to the Lord your God. Do not mourn or weep. For all the people had been weeping as they listened to the words of the Law…The Levites calmed all the people, saying, Be still, for this is a sacred day. Do not grieve. Then all the people went away to eat and drink…and to celebrate with great joy, because they now understood the words that had been made known to them." There's the important key for any preaching of the Word of God - they were able "to celebrate with great joy, because they now understood the words that had been made known to them." Do you have a time of celebration and praise as you read the Word of God? As the Holy Spirit exercises his ministry in your soul and life, does it cause you to rejoice and to be filled with joy. This is a unique response. On the one hand, John 16:7-14 is taking place, namely, The Holy spirit "…will convict the world concerning sin and righteousness and judgment…He will declare to you the things that are to come. He will glorify me, for he will take what is mine and declare it to you." On the other hand, Galatians 5:22-23 is also taking place, namely, the production of spiritual fruit – "…the fruit of the Spirit is love, joy, peace, patience, kindness, goodness, faithfulness, gentleness, self-control;…If we live by the Spirit (by His enablement), let us also walk by the Spirit." Apart from the ministry of the Holy Spirit, nothing significant will occur in the culture, the nation or the "church".

Nehemiah has two more matters for the people to consider and decide upon. First: Nehemiah 9:5-8 - The direction for the people, namely, what they need to do in terms of their relationship to the Lord. He wrote: "Stand up and praise the LORD your God, Who is from everlasting to everlasting. Blessed be Your glorious name, and may it be exalted above all blessing and praise. You alone are the Lord. You made the heavens, even the highest heavens, and all their starry host, the earth and all that is on it, the seas and all that is in them. You give life to everything, and the multitudes of heaven worship You. You are the Lord God, who chose Abram and brought him out of Ur of the Chaldeans and named him Abraham. You found his heart faithful to you, and you made a covenant with him..." They need to know and understand the Covenant God has established with His people and the implications of that Covenant to His people in all generations. The "church" today would do well to remember that truth and application as reiterated in Galatians 3:29, "And if you are Christ's, then you are Abraham's offspring, heirs according to promise." The New Living Translation renders this verse, "And now that you belong to Christ, you are the true children of Abraham. You are his heirs, and now all the promises God gave to him belong to you." It is an everlasting Covenant established by God as He purposes to be in relationship with them. He is The One Who dictates the terms of the Covenant and man cannot amend or alter it in any way. The stipulations are God's alone.

The Second matter pertains to: The agreement of and by the people before The Holy God. In Nehemiah 9:38, Nehemiah is leading the people into a positional and relational acknowledgement of Who God is and what duty requires of them. They must learn and acknowledge: (a) They are the covenant people of God, and (b) The Covenant-Originator – The Lord Himself – Has His list of particulars to which the covenant people must adhere to obediently, affirm and implement. As the people are challenged to live according to their high calling by God, they respond in a very sweeping and comprehensive manner. Their response is: "In view of all this, we are making a binding agreement, putting it in writing, and our leaders, our Levites and our priests are affixing their seals to it."

In Nehemiah 10:28-37, The detailed/particular agreement is attested to by all. "The rest of the people–priests, Levites, gatekeepers, singers, temple servants and all who separated themselves from the neighboring peoples for the sake of the Law of God, together with their wives and all their sons and daughters who are able to understand–all these now join their brothers the nobles, and bind themselves with a curse and an oath to follow the Law of God given through Moses the servant of God and to obey carefully all the commands, regulations and decrees of the Lord, our Lord. They sign the following terms of agreement before the Lord - - -

1.   We promise not to give our daughters in marriage to the peoples around us or take their daughters for our sons.

2.   When the neighboring peoples bring merchandise or grain to sell on the Sabbath, we will not buy from them on the Sabbath or on any holy day. Every seventh year we will forgo working the land and will cancel all debts.

3.   We assume the responsibility for carrying out the commands to give a third of a shekel each year for the service of the house of our God: for the bread set out on the table; for the regular grain offerings and burnt offerings; for the offerings on the Sabbaths, New Moon festivals and appointed feasts; for the holy offerings; for sin offerings to make atonement for Israel; and for all the duties of the house of our God.

4.   We – the priests, the Levites and the people–have cast lots to determine when each of our families is to bring to the

house of our God at set times each year a contribution of wood to burn on the altar of the Lord our God, as it is written in the Law.

5.   We also assume responsibility for bringing to the house of the Lord each year the first-fruits of our crops and of every fruit tree. As it is also written in the Law, we will bring the firstborn of our sons and of our cattle, of our herds and of our flocks to the house of our God, to the priests ministering there.

6.   Moreover, we will bring to the storerooms of the house of our God, to the priests, the first of our ground meal, of our [grain] offerings, of the fruit of all our trees and of our new wine and oil.

7.   And we will bring a tithe of our crops to the Levites, for it is the Levites who collect the tithes in all the towns where we work..

8.   Finally, Nehemiah 10:39, their clear commitment and focus both to and before the Lord - "We will not neglect the house of our God."

Such an agreement to which they committed themselves to adhere to and implement immediately requires a prayer commitment as well. Psalm 77:1-15 is a fine guideline for such a prayer commitment as they begin their journey of Remembering, Repenting and Returning to The Lord. They are in the process of getting themselves turned around and getting back on track with The Lord. The Psalmist prays a prayer that can be used as a model prayer for those who are Taking a Serious God Seriously. "I cried out to God with my voice...And He gave ear to me. In the day of my trouble I sought the Lord; My hand was stretched out in the night without ceasing; My soul refused to be comforted. I remembered God, and was troubled; I complained, and my spirit was overwhelmed. You hold my eyelids open; I am so troubled that I cannot speak. I have considered (remembered) the days of old, The years of ancient times. I call to remembrance my song in the night; I meditate within my heart, And my spirit makes diligent search. (a) Will the Lord cast off forever? (b) And will He be favorable no more? (c) Has His mercy ceased forever? (d) Has His promise failed forevermore? (e) Has God forgotten to be gracious? (f) Has He in anger shut up His tender mercies?" The Psalmist needed to remember that God is not like men. He is never in a vacuum and He is always eager to respond to the soul that seeks Him. As one begins to pray to the Lord and make commitments to Him, it would be wise to have before one the words of Jeremiah 29:11-14, "For I know the plans I have for you, declares the Lord, plans for welfare and not for evil, to give you a future and a hope. Then you will call upon me and come and pray to me, and I will hear you. You will seek me and find me, when you seek me with all your heart. I will be found by you, declares the Lord, and I will restore your fortunes and gather you from all the nations and all the places where I have driven you, declares the Lord, and I will bring you back to the place from which I sent you into exile." These words are the Covenant-Originator's – The Lord Himself - words spoken to encourage one to persist in seeking Him with all of one's heart.

The Psalmist continued his prayer: "And I said, this is my anguish; but I will remember the years of the right hand of the Most High. I will remember the works of the Lord; Surely I will remember Your wonders of old. I will also meditate on all Your work, And talk of Your deeds. Your way, O God, is in the sanctuary; Who is so great a God as our God? You are the God who does wonders; You have declared Your strength among the peoples. You have with Your arm redeemed Your people..." This prayer journey involves one remembering God – all of Who He is and all of what He has done (and continues to do). It also involves one in meditation upon God and His Word to His people. The culture, nation and the "church" also needs to remember the basic truth and moral value stated in Psalm 1:1-2, " Blessed is the man who walks not in the counsel of the wicked, nor stands in the way of sinners, nor sits in the seat of scoffers; but his delight is in the law of the Lord, and on his law he meditates day and night." The value and advantage to meditating upon God's Word "day and night" is that one begins to own God's Word in and for one's life. My Maternal Grand-mother was born in Scotland and migrated to the United States in the early 1900s. One of the memories I have of her was her knowledge and use of the Bible in her life. After she had died, a Jewish merchant with whom she had done business stopped by and inquired about her and that he missed seeing her. When I told him that she had died, he reflected what a fine woman she was and that he looked forward to her coming into his store every day because she always had a Bible verse that she shared with him. This usage of God's Word can only come as a result of meditating in it day and night. She also had many pithy sayings that she employed frequently. I still remember her looking directly into my eyes and reminding me as I went out to play (or to get into some mischief) – "Remember – Thou God seest me!" I think she must've gleaned it from Genesis 16:13, "Then she (Hagar) called upon the name of the Lord who spoke to her, You-Are-the-God-Who-Sees; for she said, Have I also here seen Him who sees me?" Are you cognizant of the God Who sees you wherever you are and is knowledgeable of whatever you are doing?

If one desires to be focused and committed to Taking A Serious God Seriously, then the idea of a personal covenant with Him would be of value. Have you ever considered writing a personal covenant and presenting it to the Lord? What kind of Covenant would it be? What kind of Covenant have you entered into with the Covenant Originator – The Lord? Is It Based Upon His Terms or Yours? How Consistent Are You In Maintaining and Following Through With The Covenant That Will Please The Lord? Is it Merely a historical or mechanical statement – or – a living document that Is part of your life and that which you reference every day?

Some time ago, Focus On The Family began a Ministry for Pastors. The idea was to have an outlet where a Pastor could speak with and seek counsel in a confidential way. One of the ministry tools developed was The Shepherd's Covenant. It is based upon the acronym G-R-A-C-E. The simple purpose for this is: "It is a strategy for moral, spiritual and ethical protection based on the guidelines practiced by the Good Shepherd." What does this agreement or covenant state as the five basic guidelines for a Shepherd's Life and Ministry.

G = Genuine Accountability — There is a great difference between being cordial and collegiate. We need colleagues in our lives who will ask us hard questions and allow us to do the same with them. "Jonathan became one in spirit with David, and he loved him as himself" (1 Samuel 18:1).

R = Right Relationships — Our ministries can only be effective when our actions and reactions toward members of our families, our colleagues in ministry, and the members of our congregations are pure. We must be clergy of peace. "Live in harmony and peace, and may the God of love and peace be with you" (2 Corinthians 13:11).

A = A Servant/Shepherd's Heart — The example that the Good Shepherd gave to His followers was in the first place that of a servant – the towel, the basin and a sincere willingness to be humble (John 14) – and in the second place that of an overseer who carefully watches his flock. "I lay down my life for the sheep" (John 10:15).

C = Constant Safeguards — We must be vigilant. To put on the whole armor of God (Ephesians 6:10) is not merely an option. It is a necessity if we are going to successfully obey the command of our Lord to flee the various onslaughts of Satan.

E = Embrace God Intimately — The deeper one's relationship with God through His Son Jesus, the more successful he will be in living a life above reproach and setting an example for the believers in speech, in life, in love, in faith and in purity (1Timothy 4:12). An intimate relationship with Him makes it all possible. "Come near to God and he will come near to you"(James 4:8).

In a similar way, each parishioner in a particular "church" can begin to influence others – not in or with a Pharisaical approach (such as, don't do as "I" do, just do as "I" say) – but in the righteous, godly and holy walk one is consistently maintaining with the Lord. A concern is that too many could not do it, whereas some others would not attempt in. The value for one attempting to put into writing his or her faith-walk goals is that it would serve as a personal check-up and an evaluation of the progress and growth that is being made. This is just one of the practical ways one can demonstrate that he/she is Taking A

Serious God Seriously. May God bless you richly in your spiritual journey with Him.

In order for one to be able to Take A Serious God Seriously, a beginning point would be the application of James 1:22-25, Do not merely listen to the word, and so deceive yourselves. Do what it says. Anyone who listens to the word but does not do what it says is like a man who looks at his face in a mirror and, after looking at himself, goes away and immediately forgets what he looks like. But the man who looks intently into the perfect law that gives freedom, and continues to do this, not forgetting what he has heard, but doing it--he will be blessed in what he does."

Chapter Thirteen contains a list of questions for self-examination. Rather than having them appear to be rhetorical, let us try to give response to them here.

1.   A place where self-examination can begin is in Prayer and Inquiry.
In Psalm 77, the Psalmist ponders his life and relationship to the Lord with intimate and particular questions. What are your thoughts and responses to the following?

- Will the Lord cast us off forever? (What has Christ come to do?)

- Will He be favorable no more? (What is the Character of God in terms of Hs Grace?)

- Has His mercy ceased forever? (How does this dove-tail with His being Longsuffering?)

- Has the promise failed forevermore? (What are all of the promises to us in Christ – II Corinthians 1:20?)

- Has God forgotten to be gracious?

- Has He in anger shut up His tender mercies (How long of a time does His anger last - Psalm 30:5?)

2. The Psalmist continues with his self-examination and pondering additional questions in Psalm 85 - - -

- Will You be angry with us forever? (Toward whom is God the most angry – Psalm 7:11?)

- Will You prolong Your anger to all generations? (Once again – for how long of a period does His anger last – Psalm 30:5?)

- Will you not revive us again, that Your people may re-joice in You? Will this longing and prayer be frustrated by the Lord?

In Psalm 119 (Read In NKJV), we find the Psalmist crying out to the Lord in terms of Revival. He wants nothing to interfere with his walk before the Lord and his fellowship with Him...
Has the "church" today reached a point where these state-ments epitomizes the heart and longing of God's people? Attach a numeric value of One for Low up to Ten for High for each of the following statements from Psalm 119. Which one's are the most relevant and urgent for today?

- Psalm 119:25 - My soul cleaves to the dust; Revive me according to Thy word.

- Psalm 119:37 - Turn away my eyes from looking at vanity, And revive me in Thy ways.
- Psalm 119:40 - Behold, I long for Thy precepts; Revive me through Thy righteousness.
- Psalm 119:50 - This is my comfort in my affliction, That Thy word has revived me.
- Psalm 119:88 - Revive me according to Thy loving-kindness, So that I may keep the testimony of Thy mouth.
- Psalm 119:93 - I will never forget Thy precepts, For by them Thou hast revived me.
- Psalm 119:107 - I am exceedingly afflicted; Revive me, O LORD, according to Thy word.
- Psalm 119:149 - Hear my voice according to Thy loving-kindness; Revive me, O LORD, according to Thine ordinances.
- Psalm 119:154 - Plead my cause and redeem me; Revive me according to Thy word.
- Psalm 119:156 - Great are Thy mercies, O LORD; Revive me according to Thine ordinances.
- Psalm 119:159 - Consider how I love Thy precepts; Revive me, O LORD, according to Thy loving-kindness.

Search me, O God, And know my heart today;
Try me, O Savior, Know my thoughts, I pray.
See if there be Some wicked way in me;
Cleanse me from every sin And set me free.

O Holy Ghost, Revival comes from Thee;
Send a revival, Start the work in me.
Thy Word declares Thou wilt supply our need;
For blessings now, O Lord, I humbly plead.

Concluding Thoughts

No one knows or is able to predict when the Bridegroom will appear and walk in the midst of His bride – The Church. For the one Taking A Serious God Seriously, there will be the expectation and preparation for his soon appearing. When one believes the Holy Scriptures, there are certain truths that are clear: (1) Jesus Christ is coming again; (b) He's coming on a day and at an hour that no one knows or is able to predict; (c) when He returns, there will be an assessment of His Church similar to Revelation 2 and 3; (d) it will be a time of both surprise and disappointment; (e) for those surprised, it will mean reward – for those disappointed, it will mean banishment from His Kingdom.

The basis by which there will be both surprise and disappointment is stated in Matthew 7:21-23, "Not everyone who says to me, 'Lord, Lord,' will enter the kingdom of heaven, but the one who does the will of my Father who is in heaven. On that day many will say to me, 'Lord, Lord, did we not prophesy in your name, and cast out demons in your name, and do many mighty works in your name?' And then will I declare to them, I never knew you; depart from me, you workers of lawlessness." A second passage is Matthew 25:31-46, "...When the Son of Man comes in his glory, and all the angels with him, then he will sit on his glorious throne. Before him will be gathered all the nations, and he will separate people one from another as a shepherd separates the sheep from the goats...Then the King will say to those on his right, 'Come, you who are blessed by my Father, inherit the kingdom prepared for you from the foundation of the world... Then he will say to those on his left, 'Depart from me, you cursed, into the eternal fire prepared for the devil and his angels...And these will go away into eternal punishment, but the righteous into eternal life." A third passage is II Thessalonians 2:7-12, "For the mystery of lawlessness is already at work. Only he who now restrains it will do so until he is out of the way. And then the lawless one will be revealed, whom the Lord Jesus will kill with the breath of his mouth and bring to nothing by the appearance of his coming. The coming of the lawless one is by the activity of Satan with all power and false signs and wonders, and with all wicked deception for those who are perishing, because they refused to love the truth and so be saved. Therefore God sends them a strong delusion, so that they may believe what is false, 12 in order that all may be condemned who did not believe the truth but had pleasure in unrighteousness."

The Holy Scriptures are clear that drastic and catastrophic times are on the horizon. It is a time that should stimulate and provoke thorough and serious self-examination. It is a time to ascertain whether or not you will be numbered with the sheep or goats. The people in Noah's day discovered that once the rain started to fall and they rushed to gain entrance into the Ark of Refuge – they had waited too long and missed their opportunity for safety and deliverance.

You have this moment! This is your day! The opportunity to get into a right and meaningful relationship with The Good Shepherd may not pass your way again. Whatever you do, make some time and space where you can purpose that you will begin Taking A Serious God Seriously. It will be the decisive time when you will either be numbered with the sheep or numbered with the goats. Your soul and eternity are at a threshold decision point. Take that step of faith now!

Made in the USA
Charleston, SC
21 March 2016

Made in the USA
Charleston, SC
21 March 2016